REVOLUTIONS

REFLECTIONS ON AMERICAN EQUALITY AND FOREIGN LIBERATIONS

THE WILLIAM E. MASSEY SR.
LECTURES IN THE HISTORY OF
AMERICAN CIVILIZATION
1989

REVOLUTIONS

REFLECTIONS ON AMERICAN EQUALITY AND FOREIGN LIBERATIONS

DAVID BRION DAVIS

HARVARD UNIVERSITY PRESS

CAMBRIDGE, MASSACHUSETTS

LONDON, ENGLAND

1990

This book is printed on acid-free paper, and its binding
materials have been chosen for strength and durability.

Library of Congress Cataloging-in-Publication Data
Davis, David Brion.
Revolutions : reflections on American equality
and foreign liberations /
David Brion Davis.
p. cm.—
(The William E. Massey Sr. lectures
in the history of American civilization)
Includes bibliographical references.
ISBN 0-674-76805-1 (alk. paper)
1. United States—History—Revolution. 1775–1783—Influence.
2. France—History—Revolution. 1789–1799—
Foreign public opinion, American.
3. Revolutions—Public opinion—History.
4. Equality—United States—History.
5. Public opinion—United States—History.
I. Title. II. Series.
E209.D38   1990
973.3—dc20   89-48924
CIP
Designed by Gwen Frankfeldt

To the Memory of Arthur M. Wilson,
a great biographer and historian,
and the teacher to whom I am most deeply indebted

ACKNOWLEDGMENTS

As a graduate of Harvard's doctoral Program in the History of American Civilization, I was both honored and deeply moved when I returned to Harvard Yard in May 1989 and delivered the Massey Lectures in a classroom in which I had long ago been instructed as a student. For this return to intellectual and institutional roots I am grateful to Stephan Thernstrom and the members of the committee responsible for the William E. Massey Sr. Lectures. It was a very special and unexpected privilege to be introduced at one of the lectures by Oscar Handlin, whose lecture course in 1952–53 transformed and enriched my understanding of American history. I felt equally honored by the generous words of my friend and coauthor, David Herbert Donald, and by the extraordinary dinner and reception given by Alan Heimert.

I would like to thank Jon Butler, Michael G. Kammen, Edmund S. Morgan, and Harry Stout for reading and commenting on early drafts of the manuscript. The helpful suggestions they made by no means imply agreement with all my arguments, and I alone am responsible for errors of fact or interpretation. Peter Hinks and Laura Mitchell gave me invaluable help in tracking down sources. An earlier version of part of the manuscript benefited from Susan Armeny's editorial suggestions. It was a delight to work with Aida D. Donald, Editor-in-Chief of Harvard University Press, and with Ann Louise C. McLaughlin, whose careful eye and acute ear are matched by sensitivity and intelligence. I am indebted to my son Adam, an accomplished cellist, for explaining how the bridge of the instrument responds to the tightening and loosening of strings. I was greatly pleased that Adam, my son Noah, and my wife, Toni, were able to come to Cambridge to hear the first lecture. As in the past, Toni helped me organize my time and gave me indispensable support and encouragement while pursuing her own professional career.

A portion of this book was used in my 1989 presidential address to the Organization of American Historians, "American Equality and Foreign Revolutions," which was published in the December 1989 issue of *The Journal of American History*.

REVOLUTIONS

REFLECTIONS ON
AMERICAN EQUALITY AND
FOREIGN LIBERATIONS

I

THE AMERICAN REVOLUTION AND THE MEANING OF EQUALITY

❧

THE BICENTENNIALS of both the American Bill of Rights and the French Declaration of the Rights of Man, preceded by contentious debates over the meaning of the French Revolution, invite us to ponder a momentous question: How are we to interpret the response of the United States, over the course of two centuries, to foreign revolutions? If we still cling to remnants of our old national messianic dream, we may ask why it is that a nation created by revolution, a nation whose first president ceremoniously received the key to the fallen Bastille as the "early trophy," in Thomas Paine's words, "of the Spoils of Despotism and the first ripe fruits of American principles transplanted into Europe"[1]—why such a nation should become in time the world's leading adversary of popular revolutions, the neo-Metternichian supporter of such reactionary leaders as Fulgencio Batista y Zaldívar of Cuba, Ferdinand Marcos of the Philippines, Mohammed Riza Pahlavi of Iran, Ngo Dinh Diem of South Vietnam, Anastasio Somoza Debayle of Nicaragua, François Duvalier of Haiti, and Augusto Pinochet Ugarte of Chile?

Framing the question in such extreme terms inevitably provokes sharp debate about the meaning and comparability of revolutions, to say nothing of economic imperialism and the objectives of American foreign policy. Still, there is abundant evidence that the "cause" of the American Revolution, as Paine put it in *Common Sense,* ceased long ago to be "the cause of all mankind." Unless, that is, we choose to regard the continuing desire of millions of people to immigrate to the United States from all quarters of the world as a kind of uncelebrated revolution in slow motion. Critics often forget that America has been less a refuge for the privileged orders than for peasants, artisans, and dissidents of various kinds who have often translated hope for a better world into flight to a promised land. Leaving this point aside, one explanation, favored by some historians on the left, is that American leaders betrayed their revolutionary principles in 1918–19, or in the 1790s, or at the Constitutional Convention, or even before independence had been won. A plausible argument has also been made that America's War of Independence was not a revolution at all, at least in the sense of a violent upheaval that changed the basic structure of society, especially what Marx called the social relations of production. Instead, on this view, America's independence confirmed trends long under way and finally freed slaveholding planters and a mercantile elite from the constraints of imperial authority.[2]

I suspect that the picture would look quite different if the British and some half-million loyalists had won the war and if we now had the benefit of scholarly therapeutic analyses supported by a Thomas Hutchinson Institute for the Study of Revolution, perhaps located at Harvard. Even in the 1770s loyalists like Hutchinson and Jonathan Boucher insisted that the rebellion had nothing to do with taxes or alleged oppressive measures. Tracing stages of subversive thought from fanatical Puritanism to the defeat of the French in 1763, which removed a "formidable Enemy" from the colonists' frontiers, the loyalists charged that a small group of demagogues and radical conspirators, imbued with "democratic, levelling principles," had plotted with debtors, smugglers, and members of the opposition party in England to overthrow the British constitution. After the zealots had intimidated Parliament and then used "every fiction, falsehood, and fraud" to inflame the public, "no one could call his Body his own," according to Peter Oliver, "for that was at the mercy of the Mob."[3]

I have no interest in considering typologies of revolution,

the kind that were popular a quarter-century ago among social scientists who identified the stages of "dysfunction" in social systems and plotted "J curves" of popular expectations soaring beyond the actual satisfaction of human needs.[4] Someday historians may wish to compare the American establishment's attempts to diagnose and prevent revolution with the New Left's romantic conviction that all revolutions were, as the saying went, "neat." Both sides thought they understood what Crane Brinton had earlier called the anatomy of revolution as well as what revolution was all about. Still drawing on Western political traditions from Plato and Hobbes to Rousseau and Marx, no one could foresee the Soviet Union's frustrations with Afghanistan and Ethiopia or the disastrous social effects of U.S.-sponsored "freedom fighters" in El Salvador and Nicaragua. In 1979, after a period of disillusion over the supposedly democratizing effects of "modernization," most liberal-minded Americans either cheered or sighed with relief when the Ayatollah Khomeini finally flew from Paris to Tehran. Few Westerners suspected, as Bernard Lewis has recently pointed out, that for modern Islamic rebels neither the French nor Russian revolution "provide[s] usable models or evocative symbols."[5]

In the late 1980s, as the meaning of revolution became increasingly ambiguous and increasingly detached from traditional bourgeois and Marxist ideology, the Soviet Union and the People's Republic of China began to reassess their own revolutionary histories, including the human and economic costs of the Chinese Cultural Revolution and the appalling crimes of Stalinism. In typical news reports we read that Mikhail Gorbachev had renounced any goal of forcibly overthrowing capitalism; that the road to socialism had been redefined to take advantage of market incentives; that in the spring of 1988 signs on factory walls in China, once emblazoned with the wisdom of Chairman Mao, proclaimed Benjamin Franklin's proverb, "Time is money"; that a year later the army in Beijing was unable to control up to one million demon-strators, organized by students and cheered and joined by fac-tory workers, who demanded democracy, symbolized by a rough replica of the Statue of Liberty, as well as an end to gov-ernmental corruption and authoritarian control, before they were finally gunned down by the People's Liberation Army.[6]

Nothing could be more fatuous than to interpret these devel-opments, culminating in the collapse of Communist govern-ments in Eastern Europe, as a prelude to the Americanization of the world.[7] But when the voters of Poland, given the first chance in over forty years to express their views in parliamen-tary elections, overwhelmingly repudiate the Communist gov-ernment that rules in their name; when the people of other Communist nations overthrow one-party despotism and strug-gle for freedom of expression, revealing a deep-seated popular longing for political and legal rights we have long defended as a legacy of the American Revolution, we can see the absurdity of the recently fashionable view that for two centuries the United States has been struggling to preserve a sclerotic Pres-ent and fight off the Future, as represented by a regenerative, revolutionary world.[8] It is well to remember that Marx himself viewed capitalism as "permanently revolutionary, tearing down all obstacles that impede the development of productive forces, the expansion of needs, the diversity of production and the exploitation and exchange of natural and intellectual forces."[9] Despite the general accuracy of this description of capitalism, few of us today can share Marx's confidence that we know where history is headed.

While I hope to convey some idea of the extraordinary com-plexity of American responses to foreign revolutions, this book will have served its purpose if it points to the kind of detailed investigations needed before we can reach a sound synthesis, a synthesis grounded in the social history of particular groups, factions, classes, and political ecologies but also illuminated by an intellectual history that discovers long-term continuities, traditions, reenactments, and symbolic meanings. As V. S. Naipaul has eloquently put it:

> There is a history in all men's lives
> Figuring the natures of the times deceased.[10]

Because this is no more than a pilot study, I have accepted the need to be highly selective, concentrating particularly on the Americans' exuberance and disillusion over the French Revolution, the success of which, Jefferson believed, was "necessary to stay up our own [government] and to prevent it from falling back to that kind of Half-way-house, the English constitution."[11]

As Jefferson's words suggest, foreign revolutions could be viewed as essential not only to further America's liberating mission abroad but to protect liberty at home. Ambassador David R. Francis appealed to Woodrow Wilson's desire to protect and extend domestic New Freedom programs, when he wrote from Russia in March 1917, calling for immediate diplomatic recognition and aid to the world's newest democracy. "This revolution," he assured Wilson, "is the practical realization of that principle of government which we have championed and advocated."[12] Foreign revolutions could play a crucial role in redefining the sources and nature of evil; in constricting or extending Americans' concepts of equality; and in changing the meaning of America's own Revolutionary tradition. No one doubts the influence of foreign revolutions on the Sedition Acts of 1798 and 1918, the great Red Scare of 1919–20, and McCarthyism. The positive contributions of foreign revolution have been less direct and are far more difficult to establish, for example, with respect to expanded suffrage, abolitionism, the acceptance of labor unions, and racial desegregation. Yet demands for domestic reform have seldom been unrelated to events abroad.

To cite only two examples: in *Uncle Tom's Cabin*, a novel of unprecedented popularity written soon after the Revolutions of 1848, Harriet Beecher Stowe warned that only the abolition of slavery might appease "the Red Revolution" and the "mustering among the masses, the world over." Barely a century later the Voice of America immediately dramatized the significance of *Brown v. Board of Education* in broadcasts aimed at Eastern Europe and Communist China. For the past two centuries nodes of tension within American society have been acutely sensitized to news that the nations of the world, as Stowe put it in 1852, were "trembling and convulsed . . . surging and heaving . . . as with an earthquake."[13] Beginning in the 1790s, American millennialist hopes strained against deeply inbred fears of tyrannical power and anarchy, fears of men either assuming godlike authority or repudiating authority altogether.

At the outset, as Edmund Burke reminds us, there is the problem of nomenclature and models. The traumatic revolution upon which Burke reflected in 1790, with its later September Massacres of 1792, regicide, Reign of Terror, Thermidor, and 18th Brumaire, became the prototype or paradigm for international revolution for at least the next one hundred and twenty-eight years. When Burke wrote, however, the word "revolution" still had joyful and comforting connotations in England and was eagerly appropriated by Americans to describe their own change of government. Drawing on the work of Karl Griewank, J. H. Elliott stresses how slowly "the idea of revolution was brought down from the heavens of Copernicus and applied with any precision to the mutations of states." Although nineteenth- and twentieth-century historians have tended to see "revolts in Early Modern Europe in the light of the late eighteenth-century revolutions," Elliott adds, the words most commonly used were "sedition, rebellion, *Aufstand,* mutation, revolt, revoltment."[14] In England the word "revolution" seldom evoked thoughts of Diggers and Fifth Monarchy Men, Pride's Purge, or the beheading of Charles I. *The* revolution, whose centennial the Revolution Society had cheerfully celebrated in a tavern, according to Burke, was England's Glorious Revolution of 1688.[15]

What made this revolution so glorious was its demonstration that a corrupt king who conspired to subvert the constitution could be induced to vacate the throne without bloodshed and without infringing on the hereditary succession of monarchs or disturbing the delicate constitutional balance that supposedly ensured political and social stability. It could hardly have been coincidental that beginning in 1775 George Washington called the defense of American liberties the "glorious cause," a judgment with which Burke essentially agreed.[16] But to Burke's horror, by November 1789 the Revolution Society and Dr. Richard Price, "a non-conforming minister of eminence," confounded the Glorious Revolution of 1688 not only with the lawless Puritan upheaval and bloodbath of the 1640s but with the "Theban and Thracian Orgies" being enacted in France. Disregarding the constitutional restraints of the 1689 Declaration of Rights, Burke pointed out, Price echoed the very phrases of the Reverend Hugh Peter, the Puritan regicide. Like the Puritan fanatic, Price rejoiced over the eradication of what he perceived as superstition and error and the spectacle of *"an arbitrary monarch surrendering himself to his subjects."*[17]

There were, in short, good revolutions and bad revolutions, lawful overturnings and anarchy. In 1789 and 1790 English and American liberals hailed the French Revolution as a fulfillment of the principles of the revolutions of 1688 and 1776. Skeptics like Burke and John Adams, both of whom had defended the American Revolution, could point to no recent examples of revolutionary anarchy.[18] To substantiate their fears they were forced to select rather remote examples from antiquity, Cromwellian England, or, in Adams' case, Enrico

Caterino Davila's account of the sixteenth-century French civil wars. As late as 1796, Raymond Williams notes, the word "revolution" could denote the positive antithesis of "rebellion"; he cites the maxim: "Rebellion is the subversion of the laws, and Revolution is that of tyrants."[19]

The English Restoration of 1660, which led to the execution of men like Hugh Peter, had been referred to as a salutary "revolution." Cromwell, according to his royalist enemies, had been engaged in "the Great Rebellion," which by later convention became the English Civil Wars. Our own Civil War was named in official government records the "War of the Rebellion," although Southerners and their later sympathizers insisted on the "War between the States." The historians Charles and Mary Beard presented a persuasive but ultimately unsuccessful case for calling the Civil War the "Second American Revolution," arguing that this "social war" established "a new power in the government, making vast changes in the arrangement of classes, in the accumulation and distribution of wealth, in the course of industrial development, and in the Constitution inherited from the Fathers."[20] That the choice of such labels matters can be shown by a simple observation: If we seriously regarded the Civil War as a revolution, the United States, for all its alleged stability and continuity, would become the scene of the Western world's bloodiest and most destructive revolution before the twentieth century.[21]

Whatever labels they eventually acquired, revolutions from the time of Aristotle and especially from the time of the English Diggers, Levelers, and Fifth Monarchy Men have been closely associated with conflicting ideas of equality. And American understandings of equality, with all their internal tension, ambiguity, and changing implications, have both shaped and been shaped by perceptions of foreign revolutions. It was Alexis de Tocqueville, after all, whose immediate noble forebears had suffered death in the Terror of 1793 and expulsion from the Chamber of Peers in the Revolution of 1830, who advanced the influential thesis that equality is the fundamental theme and characteristic of American civilization.[22] Since few keywords have generated such confusion and controversy, it is important to examine some of the historical meanings of equality with great care.

Fifty years ago Georges Lefebvre wrote that "for the French of 1789 liberty and equality were inseparable, almost two words for the same thing; but had they been obliged to choose, it is equality that they would have chosen." When the mass of peasants rejoiced in their own liberation, he explained, "they were in fact thinking of the disappearance of the authority of the manorial lord, and his reduction to the status of a mere citizen."[23] Lefebvre's statement about equality would seem to get to the very heart of the difference between the French and American revolutions. Today most Americans, I suspect, would find it extremely difficult to understand how liberty and equality could be inseparable or "almost two words for the same thing." The conundrum might be explained by expanding upon Lefebvre's reference to peasants and a feudal lord. It is extremely difficult for Americans to imagine the deference and inferiority people must have felt when kneeling before an authoritarian king or nobleman. Liberation from the hereditary inequalities of an "un-American" feudal regime might appear to merge freedom and equality, at least for a time. The American creed of equality, Edmund S. Morgan has argued, "did not give men equality, but invited them to claim it, invited them, not to know their place and keep it, but to seek and demand a better place."[24]

This line of reasoning may help to explain why the word "equality" does not appear in the American Bill of Rights or in the original Constitution itself, except in Article V, which prohibits any amendment that denies a state, without its consent, "of its equal suffrage in the Senate." This explicit denial of proportional representation is linked with an unamendable guarantee allowing states to import slaves without congressional prohibition for another twenty years. As numerous historians have argued, the creation of practical law required that abstract Revolutionary principles be filtered through a slaveholder's prism.[25]

Yet in a speech in 1856 at a Republican party banquet in Chicago, Abraham Lincoln could assert that American government rested on public opinion, that public opinion on any subject "always has a *'central idea,'* from which all its minor thoughts radiate." And, according to Lincoln, "that 'central idea' in our political opinion, at the beginning was, and until recently has continued to be, 'the equality of men.'" Speaking as if these statements were incontrovertible, he went on to demand a reinauguration of this basic principle: "The human heart *is* with us—God is with us. We shall again be able not to declare, that 'all States as States, are equal,' nor yet that 'all citizens as citizens are equal,' but to renew the broader, better declaration, including both these and much more, that 'all *men* are created equal.'"[26]

Lincoln seemed to equate being equal, the essential and continuing equality of men, with being created equal. In a close analysis of Jefferson's original wording of the equality clause in the Declaration of Independence, Morton White argues convincingly that the "logical substructure" owes much to John Locke and Jean Jacques Burlamaqui. For our purposes the precise lines of intellectual influence are less important than White's gloss "that because God endowed all men with *one* sort of equality, they should be treated or regarded as possessing *another* sort of equality." The first proposition in Jefferson's original draft, which seems clearer logically than the revised draft adopted by Congress, reads: "We hold these truths to be sacred & undeniable; that all men are created equal & independant." Following Locke, White interprets this to mean

God created all men as members of the same species, with the same basic nature. Neither Locke nor Jefferson meant "to imply that all men are equal in size, strength, understanding, figure, moral accomplishments, or civil accomplishments."[27]

In the original draft Jefferson went on to write: "that from that equal creation they derive rights inherent & inalienable, among which are the preservation of life, & liberty, & the pursuit of happiness; that to secure these ends, governments are instituted among men, deriving their just powers from the consent of the governed." Drawing again on Locke's more detailed explanation, White converts Locke's proposition into a "because" statement: "Because all men have been created equal in the sense of having been given the same nature and the same advantages, they should also be treated as equal in the sense that no one of them should depend on the will of any other man."[28] The second or derivative meaning of equality pertains to the *way* people are treated, to our universal obligation to treat men as moral and rational beings endowed with inherent rights to life, liberty, and the pursuit of happiness. For Locke, White points out, equal treatment in this sense did not conflict with the precedence that should be shown "to those who are greater in age, merit, or excellency of parts." Yet conservatives like John Adams feared that if suffrage qualifications were lowered, the principles of the American Revolution would be misunderstood: "New claims will arise; women will demand a vote; lads from twelve to twenty-one will think their rights not enough attended to; and every man who has not a farthing, will demand an equal voice with any other, in all acts of state."[29]

The colonists' early proclamations of equality, including the immortal declaration that "all men are created equal," were largely intended to assert the Americans' equality with Englishmen, who were not being taxed or subjected to search and seizure by a government in which they had no representatives, at least according to the theory of "virtual representation."[30] The Declaration of Independence, before assuring all readers and listeners that they were intelligent enough to intuit the truth that all men were created equal, affirmed the colonists' determination "to assume, among the powers of the earth, the separate and equal station to which the laws of nature and of nature's God entitle them." This meaning of equality persisted in rhetoric opposing various kinds of imperialism and demanding the right of self-government. But many colonists meant something more when they claimed, like David Ramsay, that the principle of equality was the very "life and soul" of republicanism. In 1776 the Virginia constitution's Declaration of Rights asserted that "all men are by nature equally free and independent." The constitutions of Pennsylvania, Vermont, and New Hampshire incorporated similar language. The Massachusetts constitution of 1780 affirmed: "All men are born free and equal, and have certain natural, essential, and unalienable rights." Although nineteenth-century judges resorted to what Robert M. Cover terms "thoroughgoing positivism and contextual sensitivity" in order to prevent this republican language from leading "into an open-ended exploration of the natural rights of slaves," the "free and equal clauses" did serve as an open-ended stimulus to reformers of every kind.[31]

Leading Tories like Jonathan Boucher recognized this threat when they condemned as dangerous demagoguery the absurd argument "that the whole human race is born equal; and that no man is naturally inferior, or in any respect subjected to another."[32] As the colonists' resistance moved beyond the line of treason, the rebels challenged the legitimacy of all monarchic rule and hereditary rank and privilege. Exhilarated by their own daring and common risk, they appealed to millennial visions and ancient republican ideals that promised to inaugurate a new era of public virtue and moral regeneration.[33]

Discussions of inequality today usually refer to disparities in income, wealth, housing, education, medical services, and other material benefits. Although these indexes of inequality are often subsumed under an abstract category of *social* treatment, they are far removed from what earlier generations meant by even social equality. To cite one significant illustration: the first example of democratic equality that shocked Tocqueville in 1831, prompting his first diary notation in America. It occurred when Judge James O. Morse introduced him to the governor of New York, "who was staying at a *boarding house* and who received us in the parlor without any ceremony whatever. Mr. Morse assured us that anyone could at any time do as we had done." As George Wilson Pierson observes, the governor of "one of the greatest territorial and political units in the United States" was lodged in the same building with humble travelers and was accessible to anyone: "no soldiers, no guards, no doormen, no formalities."[34]

To recapture this personal and psychological meaning of equality, we must remember two elementary points: first, it took many centuries before rank became simply another commodity that could be purchased like a horse or slave; second, ideals of equal treatment were long derived from the Bible. In the Hebrew Bible a kind of equality is implied in God's commands: "Love your neighbor as yourself"; "You and the stranger shall be alike before the Lord"; "The stranger who resides with you shall be to you as one of your citizens; you shall love him as yourself, for you were strangers in the land of Egypt."[35] In the Sermon on the Mount, Jesus translates this message into the Golden Rule: "Therefore all things whatsoever ye would that men should do to you, do ye even so unto them: for this is the law and the prophets."[36] These ideal laws of fraternity and equivalent worth were of course desiccated in effect by the hellish heat of Original Sin and the inevitability of evil—doctrines used to explain and justify every form of inferiority and oppression, despite the often suicidal efforts of perfectionist and millennialist sects who claimed to have freed themselves from sin's dominion. The Quakers, who were much admired by French philosophes, sought a middle ground between equal respect and an acceptance of fortuitous disparities in wealth and rank. As Robert Barclay tried to reassure King Charles II, the Friends were not Levelers even though they believed that men were *"alike by creation"* and condemned the idolatry of using such titles as *"Your Holiness, Your Majesty, Your Excellency . . . Your Lordship, My Lord* Peter, *My Lord* Paul," and refused to kneel, bow, uncover their heads, or prostrate themselves before fellow human beings.[37]

When America's Revolutionary leaders talked of inequality, they usually referred to relations between people, not to a fixed, historical condition. For anyone vaguely familiar with the Bible, inequality had first appeared in human history in the sibling rivalry between Adam and Eve's two sons. When Cain and Abel sought to win the Lord's favor by bringing Him competitive offerings, God ignored Cain and rewarded Abel with special esteem. Outraged by this "incongruity between destiny and merit," to use Max Weber's definition of the problem of evil, Cain made matters worse for himself by killing his brother. Apart from the narrative's fascinating implications regarding competing modes of production and ways of life (pastoral and agricultural), Cain's revolution introduced violence as a means of redress. Murder, if we reflect upon it, is the ultimate and irreversible demonstration of inequality, since it reduces a human being, a whole world of consciousness, to nonbeing.[38] Although revolutionaries often have exulted in bloodshed as a form of therapy or sacrificial purification, this illusory cure has almost always metastasized and then perpetuated the very malignancy that radicals intended to root out. There is an important difference between representing inequality as an interpersonal relationship characterized either by servile subordination or by parading triumphantly with someone's head stuck on a pike—and perceiving inequality as a historical condition created, as in Rousseau's account, when the first man enclosed a piece of land and said, *"This is mine."* It is true that Rousseau traced institutionalized inequalities to interpersonal acts of plunder and fraud. Yet for him emancipation from such historical enslavement depended, not on retaliatory efforts to plunder the plunderers, but on subjugating each individual to a transcendent and apolitical General Will.[39] Although relatively few Americans had read Rousseau, the French Revolution made them increasingly aware that attempts to right historical wrongs could easily lead to new forms of interpersonal tyranny. The problem of legitimating violence and inequality was especially poignant in a republican society based to a large extent on the labor of slaves.

Most literate Americans were familiar with biblical theodicies that explored the spiraling consequences of favoritism, jealousy, and dirty tricks, such as the story of the sale of young Joseph into slavery by his jealous brothers. Because of Joseph's arrogant treatment of his less favored brothers, they first decided to kill him and then sold him to slave traders for twenty pieces of silver. For that act, Americans knew, the brothers were later humbled before Joseph's feet. The archetype of illegitimate inequality, as Samuel Sewall argued in 1700 in his antislavery tract, *The Selling of Joseph*, was the relation between master and slave. The model was observable, close at hand. "As I would not be a *slave*," Lincoln wrote in the 1850s, "so I would not be a *master*. This expresses my idea of democracy. Whatever differs from this, to the extent of the difference, is no democracy."[40] We are so accustomed to thinking of *freedom* as the antithesis of slavery that we usually fail to see elements of bondage in any nominally free relationship that is based on inequality. Indeed, the continuing liberal emphasis on abstract freedom long diverted attention from the bondage of unequal relationships, such as those finally discovered in traditional marriage and total dependency on wage-earning employment.

"The whole commerce between master and slave," as Jefferson described the most extreme form of inequality short of torture and death, "is a perpetual exercise of the most boisterous passions, the most unremitting despotism on the [one] part, and degrading submission on the other." Or as George Mason, another Virginia planter, wrote in 1774, two years before he drafted Virginia's Declaration of Rights: "Practised in the Arts of Despotism and Cruelty, we become callous to the Dictates of Humanity, & all other finer feelings of the Soul. Taught to regard a part of our Species in the most abject & contemptible Degree below us, we lose that Idea of the Dignity of Man, which the Hand of Nature had implanted in us, for great & useful purposes. . . . Habituated from our Infancy to trample upon the Rights of human Nature, every generous, every liberal Sentiment, if not extinguished, is enfeebled in our Mind. And in such an infernal School are to be educated our future Legislators and Rulers."[41]

Mason's "infernal School" prevented even the enlightened legislators of his generation from taking effective action to eliminate slavery, despite Jefferson's apocalyptic prophecies, following the blacks' triumph in Saint Domingue, about becoming "the murderers of our own children" or being forced, "after dreadful scenes and sufferings to release [the slaves] in their own way."[42] Nevertheless, Landon Carter was probably not the only Southern planter who wondered, as soon as he read the Declaration of Independence, whether its commitment to equality and liberty meant that the slaves would have to be freed.[43] By 1787 slavery had been outlawed in Vermont, Massachusetts, New Hampshire, and the Northwest Territories, while legislation had ensured its gradual extinction in Pennsylvania, Connecticut, and Rhode Island.

Meanwhile, whatever embarrassment white colonists may

have felt regarding their treatment of blacks, the Declaration had affirmed their determination to prevent the British government from carrying out its tyrannical design to enslave *them*. As Bernard Bailyn demonstrated long ago, this talk of being enslaved was not hyperbole or lurid rhetoric; it expressed a genuine fear of being subjected, in the words of one typical writer, to "the arbitrary will and pleasure of another." According to traditional Lockean doctrine, as soon as any man was deprived of his property without consent and compensation, he had no protection against slavelike dependence. Americans had long been nourished on an ideology that led them to believe that they were being reduced, as Bailyn puts it, to the political condition "characteristic of the lives of contemporary Frenchmen, Danes, and Swedes as well as of Turks, Russians, and Poles."[44]

This fear of enslavement helps to elucidate the Founders' understanding of equality, which by 1789 became a crucially important standard for interpreting foreign revolution. America's Revolutionary leaders did not believe that men were born with equal talents and endowments, or that governments should take from the rich and give to the poor, or even that all adult males should be entitled to vote or hold office. Despite sharp differences of opinion regarding black slavery, they did generally believe that since all people were equally human before their Creator—equal in moral responsibility and vulnerability to corruption and error—they were entitled to equal respect as human beings regardless of differences in talent, wealth, and achievement. Accordingly, it was wrong both ethically and politically to treat individuals either as infallible demigods, endowed with unlimited power, or as contemptible objects, mere instruments of another's will. Governor George Clinton's backers asserted in New York's hotly contested election of 1789 that, while "the merit of no man is to be depreciated because he is rich," neither "are any to be despised because they are poor"; "we neither wish to see men of dangerous wealth or dependent poverty in office."[45]

The danger inherent in exalted rank, titled nobility, or even excessive wealth abutting grievous poverty lay in the almost irresistible delusions of superiority which, even if softened by paternalism and charity, tended to destroy what Mason termed "that Idea of the Dignity of Man" that had been implanted in human nature "for great and useful purposes." The creation of a proletariat, of dependent masses who owned no property, who could be exploited, manipulated, and scorned as the *canaille*, to use Jefferson's contemptuous French term for the rabble, obviously led to the same fatal evil. In 1789 the geographer Jedidiah Morse expressed a widespread mythic ideal when he wrote that New Englanders were mostly frugal, independent farmers who had "no overgrown capital, in which to learn profligacy of manners."[46]

For a time attacks on the luxury, self-indulgence, and social pretensions that had accompanied the drift toward aristocracy in the American colonies were coupled with demands for greater economic equality. "Above all," Drew R. McCoy writes, "this republican American was to be characterized by an unprecedented degree of social equality, whereby even the poorest man would at least be secure, economically competent, and independent. Indeed, the United States was to be a revolutionary society precisely because it would not have the permanent classes of privileged rich and dependent poor that Americans associated with the 'old' societies of mercantilist Europe. Such was the republican dream, a utopia anchored to westward expansion and free trade."[47]

Edmund S. Morgan points out that, when Connecticut reformers called for a moratorium on the payment of debts during the depression of the 1780s, opponents did not argue against the desirability of fostering a greater equality of property but claimed that this particular measure would not achieve the mutually desired goal.[48] Yet, as Gordon Wood shrewdly observes, in Revolutionary America, "the simultaneous hunger for and hatred of social pretension and distinction could be agonizingly combined in the same persons." Wood and other historians have rightly emphasized the material or economic dimension to the Revolutionary ideal of equality—the problematic belief, rooted in the widespread ownership of land and absence of feudal ranks and privilege, "that equality of opportunity would necessarily result in a rough equality of station." But the crucial point, as I have already tried to suggest, concerns the effects of equality on human relationships, the ethical and psychological consequences implied in Wood's phrase about simultaneous hunger for and hatred of distinction. In America, Morgan observes, this meant that "in order to argue for special privilege . . . it was necessary to show—and it sometimes required considerable legerdemain—that special privilege was somehow the outcome of equality or a device to protect equality."[49]

Despite their theoretical opposition to hereditary privilege, most of the Revolutionary leaders feared democracy, or at least the social convulsions that could be the likely result of such an unstable form of government. The means or methods of reducing gross inequality were therefore at least as important as the goal. Once the crust of social distinction had been broken, removing the illusion of inevitability, an entire populace could become inflamed with greed for wealth and power, like looters sacking a city struck by a flood or hurricane. Far from promoting the mutual respect of genuinely equal relations, such literal leveling could unleash an ambition in each individual to outdo and subjugate his neighbor. Or, no less ominous, as history had repeatedly shown, tyrants would emerge in the guise of self-appointed agents of the people, advancing their own fortunes by vilifying or even annihilating those who could be stigmatized as enemies of the people—the populist counterpart to the "corruption of blood" attached to treason in monarchic nations. Indeed, John Adams and other patriots had exploited such populist, defamatory techniques against Thomas Hutchinson, the Tory governor of Massachusetts.[50] It seems probable that the Revolutionary leaders were especially sensitive to the dangers of demagoguery precisely because of their own success in destroying the reputations of men who were often no less liberal or public-spirited than themselves.[51]

Merging a Puritan ethic with classical republican theory and lessons learned from the history of Greek and Roman republics, most of the Founders shared the premise that human nature exhibits at all times and places a quest for power and dominion, an inclination to usurp the authority of God, to create a party of sycophants and henchmen, and to degrade vulnerable victims to the status of animals. American colonists thought they had seen proof of this sad truth in the behavior of British leaders and their American puppets, representatives of the freest governments on earth. Over a generation ago American progressives were troubled when writers like Richard Hofstadter and Reinhold Niebuhr rediscovered elements of Calvinist and Hobbesian realism in the Founders' views of power, a sober realism that has not been dispelled, I am afraid, by the tyrannies, revolutions, counterrevolutions, and exterminations of the past sixty years.[52]

If the nation's Founders exaggerated the dangers of democracy and the virtues of a natural hierarchy, they were at least candid in acknowledging the tension between the goal of reducing inequalities and the social forces that tend to produce new or greater inequalities, including forces that claim to favor equality. Given their sense of the hazards as well as promise of revolutionary change, they would no doubt have understood Mikhail S. Gorbachev's cautionary remark in response to popular excitement over the Soviet election of March 26, 1989:

"We must not commit stupidities, attempt great leaps forward, or overreach ourselves because we could put the people's future at risk."[53] This caution, however, tended to evaporate in the millennial radiation reflected by the French Revolution.

On a global scale it is helpful to picture the struggle for greater equality being enacted along a vertical axis running from kings, dictators, and tycoons who impersonate God down to the slave, proletarian, prostitute, or political prisoner who is treated as a contemptible and disposable object. Any society's profile of relative justice and equality could be plotted along this vertical spectrum, with the elevation of one group, such as American whites, sometimes depending on the debasement of another group, such as American blacks. Intersecting this axis of power, respect, and degradation is a temporal line that extends from the Garden of Eden or Hobbesian state of nature toward a messianic age, millennium, or utopia. Yet, according to one classical and nonlinear view, we are trapped in the middle of this diagram on a cyclical Ferris wheel, destined periodically to rise toward greater freedom, equality, and virtue and then fall toward corruption, anarchy, and enslavement to tyrants. We might mistake the uplift phase of the cycle for progressive movement along the horizontal, temporal axis, especially if our ideology screened out the oppressive costs of our seeming advance. By the same token, a period of seeming retrogression might be part of a spiral movement that actually leads toward the millennium or, in secular terms, toward a more just and egalitarian world.

Faith that history may actually lead to such a better world has been a potent stimulus to social criticism and improvement, an indispensable weapon against fear, complacency, and injustice. But the tension between millennial perfection and present reality requires constant readjustment or tuning, as the vertical axis slides ahead into indeterminate time. If the tension becomes too great, as on a cello, the bridge bends backward and the strings finally snap. This is the familiar situation when revolutionaries approve the annihilation of any present reality in the pursuit of a messianic ideal. As Sergei G. Nechayev put it, the authentic revolutionary must purge himself of all pity, love, and tender feelings, learning to live day and night for "one single purpose: merciless destruction. To attain this goal, tirelessly and in a cold-blooded fashion, he must always be prepared to be destroyed and to destroy with his own hands everything that hinders its attainment."[54] But if the better world seems too remote or chimerical, or if apologists succeed in idealizing the present order, the cello strings slacken until complacent flat notes give way to silence.

In the United States political leaders seemed uncertain whether equality was an imperfect approximation, an equilibrium to be preserved, or, as Jefferson and Lincoln maintained, a promise to be gradually fulfilled.[55] During the Revolutionary and Confederation periods, American definitions of acceptable equality vacillated as Pennsylvania and other states swung toward more conservative constitutions and as state and federal governments responded slowly and reluctantly to demands from Western settlers for equal power. Among the greatest challenges, beginning in 1789, were foreign revolutions that soon revealed different understandings of equality, evil, and collective progress.

As Americans became increasingly committed to the ideal of equal opportunity, the great unacknowledged question was exemplified by Lincoln's complacent statement in 1856 that the American public had "always submitted patiently to whatever of inequality there seemed to be as a matter of actual necessity," while public politics made "a steady progress toward the practical equality of all men."[56] Did the key qualifiers "necessity" and "practical" imply that the equality of some Americans, such as upwardly mobile white males, depended in some dialectical way on a comparison with an inferior Other?

During Reconstruction, it is important to note, freed slaves demanded to be addressed as "Mr. and Mrs.," and in Southern cities they often taunted whites with such remarks as "we's all equal now." This hunger for dignity and esteem, dismissed by whites as insolence and insubordination, pointed to the subtle but essential connection between being equal and free. As the black minister Henry M. Turner put it: "If I cannot do like a white man I am not free."[57]

Frantz Fanon once wrote: "The Negro is comparison. . . . Whenever he comes into contact with someone else, the question of value, of merit, arises. . . . The question is always whether he is less intelligent than I, blacker than I, less respectable than I. Every position of one's own, every effort at security, is based on relations of dependence, with the diminution of the other. It is the wreckage of what surrounds me that provides the foundation for my virility."[58]

Fanon, drawing on Hegel's famous paradigm of the master and slave, was referring to twentieth-century revolutions against white colonialism. Ironically, it was in response to the first of these anticolonial racial wars that the United States adopted a policy of national self-interest that contradicted its own racial ideology. Since I began by referring to America's recent support of counterrevolutionary regimes in the Third World, it is appropriate to conclude by noting that in the late 1790s, when the Adams administration was waging unofficial war against Revolutionary France and suppressing domestic dissent, strategic concerns took precedence over white supremacy. Alexander Hamilton and Gouverneur Morris, America's minister in Paris, had earlier resisted the attempts of the Revolutionary French government to use America's treaty obligations and financial debt to France as a means of defending French power in the Caribbean. The United States, as a slaveholding nation threatened by the contagion of black insurrection, might conceivably have joined the French, Spanish, or

English efforts to pacify Saint Domingue and restore the slave regime. In the late 1790s, however, after France had vainly tried to maintain control of the colony by emancipating the slaves, the Adams administration praised Toussaint Louverture, signed a tripartite treaty with him and the British, and provided his army with essential arms and provisions that helped him defeat his mulatto rival, André Rigaud, and win de facto independence from France. American armed ships even bombarded Rigaud's forces, protected Toussaint's small fleet, and ferried some of his troops to the southern front. For reasons of national self-interest, the Federalist American government actually urged Toussaint to declare independence. It should be emphasized that after Haiti finally won its independence in 1804, no American administration dared to recognize the Republic until the Civil War.[59] The fact remains that America's first significant intervention in a foreign revolution helped to create a citadel of black pride that threatened the security of slaveholders throughout the Western Hemisphere. There are hints that this aid to Toussaint, the world's first black revolutionary hero, may have been made easier by the Northern Federalists' contempt for Republican slaveholders who preached the equality of man.

II

AMERICA, FRANCE, AND THE ANXIETIES OF INFLUENCE

❧

I N THE FIRST CHAPTER I examined various views of equality in the period of the American Revolution, a war fought not simply for liberty but to prevent Americans from being subjected to some kind of slavery, which is the most extreme form of inequality short of death that human beings can inflict upon other human beings. Following the leads of Jefferson and Lincoln, to say nothing of philosophers from Hobbes and Locke to Hegel and Marx, I suggested that it is really a fully acknowledged equality with the master or master class, not simply freedom, that stands as the antithesis of slavery. A manumited slave may well be free, but many generations are often required before increasing equality begins to overcome the stigma of degradation and dishonor entailed by bondage.[1] Like other abstract concepts, equality can have diverse and conflicting meanings, especially as it is extended to interpersonal relationships long accepted as part of a changeless cosmic order. For this very reason a nation founded in revolution and dedicated, as Lincoln said, to the proposition that all men are created equal, became acutely sensitive to the way other revolutions confirmed or challenged the ideological balance Americans tried to maintain between an existing social order and dreams of a better world.

In January 1794, about two weeks before the French Convention abolished slavery in the French colonies and extended the rights of citizenship to all men regardless of color, the Massachusetts Constitution Society proclaimed that the French people were struggling to destroy aristocracy and vindicate the "Equal Rights of Men." According to these Boston Republicans, the present form and methods of the

French government were matters of little concern, since "on the accomplishment of the great objects of their Revolution, depends not only the future happiness and prosperity of Frenchmen, but in our opinion of the *whole World of Mankind*."[2] Democratic-Republican political societies issued similar declarations from Federalist New England to Charleston, South Carolina. The Charleston Society even sent a petition for membership to the Jacobin Club at Paris, which after a short debate adopted the South Carolinians.[3]

During the years of the French Revolution, Americans profited from the world's freest and most fully developed press, which at this time devoted more space to foreign than to domestic news. The first reports of the fall of the Bastille appeared in American newspapers in mid-September; by late October many papers were printing and applauding the Declaration of the Rights of Man. Republican newspapers such as the *New York Journal* warned that most of the news about events from France came by way of England: "Our information comes from such a polluted source, that the small portion of truth, which is told, is so distorted and disguised as to become falsehood."[4] For the first five years of the Revolution, according to Gary B. Nash, the printed sermons of the American clergy gave virtually unanimous approval to the Revolutionary cause. Even Jedidiah Morse, the New England Calvinist who would lead the Francophobe crusade in the late 1790s, called the French cause "unquestionably good" in a Thanksgiving Day sermon of 1794 that offered excuses and optimistic explanations for the massacres, "the rejection of the Christian Religion," and other "errors and irregularities" that would cease once France had defeated her external enemies.[5]

This ardent public support of the French Revolution, long encouraged by prominent merchants, entrepreneurs, slaveholding planters, religious leaders, and state and city officials, seemed little affected by the National Convention's appropriation of centralized and unchecked political power; by the execution of a king who had once been toasted and celebrated as America's savior; by the abolition of Christianity and the worship of God; by the massacre of hundreds of thousands of peasant men, women, and children in the Vendée, Loire-Inférieure, and Maine-et-Loire; or by the Reign of Terror, which, while diminished by modern historians accustomed to twentieth-century standards of slaughter, took almost twice as many lives as the United States lost in all the battles of the War of Independence and the War of 1812 combined.[6]

John Adams, a Revolutionary leader who had once called for the eradication of all artificial social distinctions and had hoped that "this many-headed beast, the people, will . . . have wit enough to throw their riders . . . [and] put an end to an abundance of tricks with which they are now curbed and bitted, whipped and spurred," later took pride in the fact that he had been the only American statesman to see from the very beginning that the French Revolution was not a "minister of grace" but a "goblin damned."[7] But why had Adams been so exceptional? We rightly think of Jefferson as one of the French Revolution's most fervent and uncompromising supporters. Yet late in 1788, when Jefferson had just read the *Federalist Essays* in Paris and had congratulated Madison for "the best commentary on the principles of government which ever was written," elucidating a plan that essentially needed only a bill of rights, he confided that the French people were unfortunately "not yet ripe for receiving the blessings to which they are entitled." One may note parenthetically that Karl Marx later delivered similar judgments regarding other backward peoples. Jefferson, stressing the need for gradual and cautious progress toward liberty, even doubted "whether the body of the nation, if they could be consulted, would accept a Habeas corpus law, if offered them by the king." Jefferson needed no instruction regarding what Adams called the "mutinous rabble of Paris" or the fact that "bodies of men as well as individuals," as he himself had written in *A Summary View* in 1774, "are susceptible of the spirit of tyranny."[8]

In view of the American leaders' fear of tyranny and the corruption of power, one would expect considerable skepticism over the French rejection of checks and balances and creation of a single, omnipotent Assembly. Drawing in part on classical republican and English Commonwealth traditions, America's constitution-makers had insisted on maintaining a protective wall between the sovereign people and the fallible representatives who governed in their name. Powers that could not be conferred to individuals, such as control over the freedom to worship, could not be delegated to a government. Even the most radical state constitutions reserved various powers to the people and provided safeguards against legislative usurpation.[9] One result of such caution of course was to protect property and existing privilege and thus limit the scope of social reform. All this said, there seems to be a striking dissonance between our picture of the United States in the 1780s—a picture that includes repeated complaints over excessive democracy, the fearful reaction against Shays's Rebellion, the Constitutional Convention, the *Federalist Essays,* and the insistence on a protective Bill of Rights—and the ecstatic American response to the French Revolution. Why did the Revolution evoke such widespread enthusiasm and so little alarm until its most violent, radical phase had receded into the past?[10]

This question deserves more extensive study.[11] With a few exceptions, historians have not correlated the chronology of the French Revolution with anti-Jacobin statements in the Federalist press, most of which appeared several years after such ghastly events as the September Massacres of 1792. Some Federalists, including New England clergymen, remained sympathetic to the French cause until conflicts over Jay's Treaty and French provocations finally forced a basic shift in perception.[12] Much attention has been given to the party warfare ignited by Hamilton's economic program and pro-English foreign policy; to the angry public demonstrations in 1795 protesting the ratification of Jay's Treaty; and to the Federalists' attempts to suppress dissent, exemplified in the Alien and Sedition Acts and in hysterical sermons warning that by 1798 American society had become infested with the dupes or conscious agents of an atheistic French conspiracy to destroy religion, justice, and free government.

But before this reaction took hold, the American people's ardent sense of fraternity with the French went beyond a partisan fear that the Hamiltonians were plotting to Anglicize and subvert the Republic. No doubt such fear of creeping monarchism and corrupting fiscal power provided a cognitive framework for interpreting the French Revolution.[13] Yet if Hamilton's opponents had been so very concerned with the dangers of tyrannical power, centralized government, and large standing armies, why would they risk linking their political fortunes with the French Convention and Directory, which were moving down the same road that Hamilton was feared to be taking? It is worth noting that the National Assembly probably had good reasons in 1792 for granting Hamilton honorary French citizenship, a privilege denied the better-known Jefferson, whose economic and political views, R. R. Palmer contends, were in some ways less revolutionary than Hamilton's.[14] In this respect it is significant that a patriotic desire to suppress the Whiskey Rebellion of 1794 could also swing sentiment behind French efforts to crush the much larger and more violent rebellion in the Vendée. As Beatrice F. Hyslop writes: "Even newspapers whose original sympathies had been with the opponents of the liquor excise now ranged themselves, in their reports on the Whiskey Rebellion in Pennsylvania, on the side of the Federal government. This same attitude was manifested in the American papers toward the

Vendéan rebels: Law and the central government of France must be upheld. This may be, in part at least, why Robespierre's public utterances were treated so respectfully in the American press."[15]

In pondering such anomalies, it is important to recapture the French Revolution's radical unpredictability. When we look backward, as historians must do, it is difficult to overcome the illusion of an inevitable and predictable sequence of events. Because of the Franco-American alliance of 1778, which opened the way for both American independence and the financial crisis that led to the French Revolution, the French political terrain was closely scrutinized by some of the most astute minds America has produced. Yet Benjamin Franklin, John Adams, and Thomas Jefferson, all of whom lived in Paris in the decade preceding 1789, agreed that a revolution was far more likely in England than in France. Franklin, who returned to the United States in 1783, considered France the most stable power in Europe. It is true that by May 1788 Jefferson, at that time United States minister to France, thought that "a revolution in their constitution seemed inevitable, unless foreign war supervene to suspend the present crisis." But in August he could assure Monroe that "this country will, within two or three years, be in the enjoyment of a tolerably free constitution, and that without it's having cost them a drop of blood. For none has yet been spilt, tho' the English papers have set the whole nation to cutting throats." On June 29, 1789, fifteen days before the storming of the Bastille, he wrote John Jay that "this great crisis being now over, I shall not have matter interesting enough to trouble you with as often as I have done lately."[16] Thomas Paine, Gouverneur Morris, Joel Barlow, and James Monroe, all of whom witnessed the Revolution at various stages, were no more prescient than Jefferson in predicting the course and outcome of events.

America's own revolution, with its accompanying religious

millennialism, prepared Americans of different social strata to express continuing jubilation over what Robert Darnton identifies as the central message of the French Revolution—"the sense of boundless possibility. . . . Possibilism against the givenness of things. . . . A conviction that the human condition is malleable, not fixed, and that ordinary people can make history instead of suffering it."[17] It was this euphoric discovery, the discovery that even the glacial kingdoms of Europe could crack and quickly melt away, that led American mechanics, tradesmen, sailors, lawyers, shopkeepers, merchants, manufacturers, farmers, and laborers to don red cockades and sing "Ca Ira!" and the "Marseillaise"; to drink endless toasts to the Rights of Man, the French Republic, and its armies battling the forces of despotism; to gather by the thousands at Philadelphia Harbor to cheer the French warship, *L'Embuscade,* as it towed in captured vessels with the British colors reversed and humbled below the flag of the French Republic.[18] In Boston and other cities Francophiles addressed one another as "citizen" or "citess" in the case of women, the latter being a symbolic gesture toward equality that stopped short of identical rights. Disdaining all titles of distinction, Republican enthusiasts toasted their fellow "Citizen George Washington." New York's Crown Street became Liberty Street; with due ceremony Bostonians transformed Royal Exchange Alley into Equality Lane and took up collections to free prisoners in the city jail. As Philadelphia's women prepared to greet the charismatic Citizen Genet, they decorated their hair, like flower children, with patriotic ribands.[19] Even thirty years later Attorney General William Wirt could write, like a modern aging veteran of the 1960s: "My breast swells, my temples throb, and I find myself catching my breath when I recall the ecstasy with which I used to join in that glorious apostrophe to Liberty in the Marseilles [sic] Hymn. . . . And then the glorious, magnificent triumphs of the arms of France, so every way worthy of her cause! O, how we used to hang over them, to devour them, to weep and to sing, and pray over these more than human exertions and victories!"[20]

Such zeal for new possibilities could also be divisive, at least by 1793. Conservative Americans remembered that on the street an overheard pro-English remark could provoke a brawl. At Tontine's, New York City's elegant coffeehouse, hundreds of Republicans gathered in the spring of 1793 to intimidate the Federalist patrons and make them toast a liberty cap on the bar. The harshest critics of the French Revolution tended to be resident Englishmen, such as the journalist William Cobbett. But when the English millennialist Charles Crawford wrote a comparatively mild anti-Jacobin treatise in 1793, he attracted no followers from the American prophetic community. Virginia's Episcopal Bishop James Madison voiced the more typical theme in 1795 when he credited God for the "great and glorious revolution" that had spread from America to France, confirming Isaiah's prophecy that tyrants "shall be chased as the chaff of the mountain before the wind." At Republican banquets radicals drank toasts to a different Mountain, the one led by Danton and Robespierre, hoping to see tyranny "chained at its foot and may the light of liberty from its summit cheer and illuminate the whole world."[21]

For a time, enthusiasm for the French Revolution appeared to offer ways of promoting harmony at home or at least of concealing divisions within American society. In 1789 and 1790 virtually all of America's leaders had felt a need for national unity following the contentious debates over constitutional ratification and the inauguration of the new Federalist government. Even John Adams, for all his pessimism concerning obstacles to freedom in the Old World, had agreed with Franklin, Paine, and Jefferson that America's "cause is the cause of all mankind" and that America's Revolutionary patriots had fought for Europe's liberty while defending their own.[22] For most Americans other than Adams and Hamilton, the revolutionary events of 1789 and 1790 proved that America's example had "kindled a flame" in France that would eventually liberate the world from monarchic and feudal despotism. Since journalists and local politicians soon discovered that the French Revolution was immensely popular among "leather-apron men" and other groups who had struggled unsuccessfully for more egalitarian reforms, leaders of various kinds demonstrated their own egalitarian and republican spirit by organizing parades and banquets and joining in toasts to the "brave Gallicans." For a time Francophilia seemed to be a safe and even providential means for representatives of some elites to show they were not really an elite but men of the people, a game Americans have been playing with themselves ever since. In the early 1790s few Americans could predict that this appeal for ideological unity would soon produce the most bitter division in early national history.

Knowledge of that internal partisan warfare, which was exacerbated by disputes over foreign policy, has obscured the deeper joy Americans shared when they believed that republicanism was beginning to spread throughout the world. Like Alexis de Tocqueville, R. R. Palmer and a few other historians have perceived the French Revolution as part of a larger movement that leapt beyond national boundaries, rousing hope and struggle from the Netherlands to Naples and from Poland to England, where the Revolution Society and London Corresponding Society provided early models for Americans.[23] Initially most Americans shared that perception and were extremely reluctant to abandon it. The news that republican principles were exportable ended their sense of isolation and helped legitimate the lawless and even treasonable cause that the Declaration of Independence had sought to defend. By 1792 it appeared that the Declaration's appeal to "the opinions of mankind" had not been in vain, that the United States would begin to gather republican allies instead of facing a contemptuous and hostile world.

In the United States, as in France itself, the Republican movement was nourished by a great diversity of local interests that cut across class lines. The Livingstons, Clintons, and other rich landlords and speculators of the Hudson Valley were as fervent in their support of the French Revolution as were the scientists and intellectuals in Philadelphia, the manufacturers who presided over the Democratic Society of the City of New York, the Westerners who rebelled against excise taxes, and the artisans and slaveholding planters of Charleston, who were the first Americans to adulate the French Convention's minister to the United States, Genet. Such groups had quite different agendas, and the ardor of the South Carolinians, for example, cooled as Jacobinism became associated with slave emancipation and slave revolt. Many Westerners, including the society of French sansculottes in St. Louis who in 1798 gave refuge to George Rogers Clark, then a brigadier-general in the army of the French Republic, were attracted to Genet's goal of "liberating" Louisiana from Spain and opening the Mississippi to American commerce.[24] The twine binding various Republican interests was a common enmity toward "Anglomen" and their aristocratic pretensions, a fear that a counterrevolutionary victory in Europe would reduce the United States to an English vassal governed by Hamiltonian sycophants and conspirators.

This mind-set made it extremely difficult for Republican political leaders to adjust to changing circumstances or to voice hidden doubts about France that would immediately be exploited by their Federalist enemies. Early in 1791, for example, Jefferson thanked George Mason for recent news about events in France. "I look with great anxiety," he confided, "for the firm establishment of the new government in France, being perfectly convinced that if it takes place there, it will spread sooner or later all over Europe." On the contrary, Jefferson warned, "a check there would retard the revival of liberty in other countries." A prime source of his anxiety, echoed by innumerable supporters of the later Russian, Chinese, and Cuban revolutions, was his certainty that bad news from France would enhance the influence of that "sect" in America, meaning the Hamiltonians, whose "heresies" had begun to threaten the experiment to "prove that men can be governed by reason." [25]

In 1793 Jefferson was initially jubilant over the public's infatuation with Genet and exclaimed in May that "all the old spirit of 1776 is rekindling." As Secretary of State, Jefferson not only misjudged Genet's headstrong character but misled the thirty-year-old French minister by revealing his own view of the secret struggles within President Washington's cabinet. Insensitive to American political realities, Genet disregarded Jefferson's cautions and assumed that he could count on the support of the Secretary of State when he challenged Washington's interpretation of neutrality and even demanded a special session of Congress to overrule the president. In private letters to Monroe and Madison, Jefferson now expressed despair over France's "calamitous" appointment of a "hot headed . . . passionate, disrespectful" minister who would "*sink the republican* interest if they do *not abandon him*." As Jefferson and Madison privately bit their nails while waiting for the French to respond to a confidential request for Genet's recall, the French minister's arrogant conduct strengthened Hamilton's hand and coincided with news of the Jacobins' triumph, the French seizure of American ships, and the execution of the queen and Girondin leaders. For the Republicans, however, the public meetings condemning Genet's insults to Washington and violations of American neutrality simply heightened the fear of creeping monarchism. In May 1794, a year after Jefferson had admonished Genet to respect the sovereign rights of the United States, the New York Democratic Society proclaimed that "he who is an enemy to the French revolution cannot be a firm republican; and therefore, though he may be a good citizen in other respects, ought not to be intrusted with the guidance of any part of the machine of government."[26] One's faith in the French Revolution was the litmus test that would reveal either ideological purity or a betrayal of the principles of America's War of Independence and the sacred mission it bequeathed.

This objectification of evil as a counterrevolutionary force that imperiled the liberation of the world leads us back to America's anomalous alliance with its former archenemy, the despotic and popish Antichrist of the French and Indian Wars. The lineaments of the Great American Enemy, the satanic enemy of free institutions, took form in the religious wars of sixteenth- and seventeenth-century England when English Protestants first pictured themselves as the Chosen People commissioned by God to outflank the Counter-Reformation by establishing expansive colonies in Ireland, North America, and the Caribbean.[27]

The enemy, whether Spanish or French, was capable of any crime in the service of his despotic king and church, since despotism by some curious alchemy created disciplined zealots who gave no thought to moral guilt or death. Most insidious, perhaps, were the satanic plots to incite black slaves to revolt and to lead Indian savages in attacks on the frontiers of Christian civilization. By the time of the French and Indian Wars, two or three generations of Huguenot refugees scattered from Charleston to Boston had authenticated the image of France as the Antichrist and Whore of Babylon, the empire of evil whose overthrow would signal the coming millennium. Despite the cosmopolitan appeal of French manners and culture, it would be difficult to exaggerate the importance of the French and Indian Wars in providing the English colonists with a sense of apocalyptic peril and a common symbolism of religious per-version and political tyranny.[28]

Beginning in 1778, however, the United States became an ally of this same Bourbon Antichrist—or, as Benjamin Franklin put it in a letter to his English friend David Hartley, America had been "*forc'd* and *driven* into the Arms of France. She was a dutiful and virtuous Daughter. A cruel Mother-in-Law turn'd her out of Doors, defamed her, and sought her Life." Once "honourably married" to France, Franklin predicted, America would "make as good and useful a Wife as she did a Daughter" to the wicked mother who would soon regret her loss. For Franklin and other patriots it was now England that stood revealed as the despotic and even popish Great American Enemy. All the same, many American Protestants must have been dismayed to learn that after the victory at Yorktown, to which the French contributed more armed forces than the Americans, the armies of both nations attended a Solemn High Mass.[29] The Americans' gratitude to France, even when coupled with the profound Anglophobia generated by the Revolutionary War, could not disguise a sense of unease and guilt over being allied with such a traditional foe and symbol of absolutist rule.

In consequence, the United States had a compelling ideo-logical interest in seeing France transformed. Even an arch-conservative like Gouverneur Morris was shocked by what he termed the depravity and extreme rottenness of the ancien régime. Paris, he wrote in 1789, "is perhaps as wicked a spot as exists." As late as December 1792, though alarmed by the radical turns and twists of the Revolution, Morris could express his love for the French people and write that he considered "the establishment of a good constitution here as a principal means, under Divine Providence, of extending the blessings of freedom to the many millions of my fellow-men who groan in bondage on the Continent of Europe."[30]

This ideological desire to reform and liberalize America's principal ally, in conformity with America's Protestant and republican image, was closely related to what William Gass has called "sacred secularities."[31] Partly because religious history has long been segregated from political history, conforming to the separation of church and state, only a few historians have recognized the religious connotations contained in the very idea of revolution. Yet the seventeenth-century English "Revolution of the Saints" was by no means the last movement to overturn a reigning theodicy and thereby redefine the sources of evil and the historical limits of human perfection. To most Anglo-American Whigs, the less radical and therefore Glorious Revolution of 1688 suggested the equilibrium and compromise of a mixed government that allowed the maximum degree of liberty compatible with human passions and the need for order. But the words "glorious" and "revolution" took on cosmic implications in 1756 when Samuel Davies, the Presbyterian leader of the Great Awakening in Virginia, predicted a decisive military victory over the French Catholic Antichrist: "However bloody and desolating this last conflict may be," he preached, "it will bring about the most glorious and happy revolution that ever was in the world."[32] Davies was referring to nothing less than the millennium, a time in which freedom from sin would become the means for harmonious equality and selfless fraternity. When the wars with France induced leading revivalists to speak of "glorious" or "extraordinary" revolutions being close at hand, the secular realm of political and military power teetered on the brink of the apocalypse. And if the world was actually approaching the threshold of sacred time and final solutions, a concern with traditional limits, distinctions, and safeguards would become quite literally irrelevant.

In the eighteenth century this millenarian side of American thought was not confined to a lunatic fringe or to what much later generations would term fundamentalists. Biblical prophecy and eschatology were taken seriously by such representatives of the American Enlightenment as Charles Chauncy, Jonathan Mayhew, Ezra Stiles, and Benjamin Rush; by Baptists, Universalists, and a few Episcopalians as well as by Congregationalists and Presbyterians. Joseph Priestley, the English chemist and radical nonconformist minister who emigrated to the United States in 1794 to escape persecution for his sympathetic views of the French Revolution, had hailed the American Revolution as a harbinger of the millennium.[33]

Biblical prophecies, especially those in the Book of Daniel and Revelation, had long provided a vocabulary for denouncing the pope, despotic kings, slavery, and other forms of worldly injustice. During the 1770s British cabinet ministers and George III became targets for the standard anti-Catholic rhetoric of Pope's Day; Thomas Paine's secular attack on "the royal brute of Great Britain" and on monarchy as "the popery of government" dovetailed with clerical allusions to the Two Beasts, Satan, and Antichrist. As predictions of cataclysmic judgment gradually gave way to visions of imminent victory and terrestrial paradise, Calvinists and theological liberals both talked of America's mission to lead the world toward a golden age of freedom and equality. In his *Observations on the Importance of the American Revolution,* the English Dissenter Richard Price foresaw an age when "the rich and poor, the haughty grandee and the creeping sycophant [would be] equally unknown."[34] Although this fervent optimism waned in the mid-1780s, millennialism provided a framework of expectancy that gave immediate meaning to the French Revolution.

For millennialists throughout the United States, the news from France cast doubt upon the perpetuity of long accepted privilege and inequality. In 1794 an anonymous South Carolinian "Hater of Tyrants" interpreted biblical prophecies in remarkably unbiblical language: a "universal fraternity" of "tolerance, liberty, and equality," he said, would soon emerge from the French struggle with European despots. As late as 1800 an anonymous "husbandman" in Troy, New York, discovered that the "seven thunders" heard in the Revelation of Saint John represented the republics that "have arisen up out of the ruins of papal and arbitrary government, and have for their basis that great principle of nature—All men are born equal and free."[35] Whether they heard the blast of the seventh angel's trumpet or saw the tree of liberty spreading its roots across Europe, millennialists and secular utopians shared a common hatred of luxury, haughty pride, and corruption as well as an impatience with compatriots who stood in the middle of the road.

In a careful study of book catalogs and lending libraries Ruth Bloch has recently found that Francophile millennialist literature was widely distributed in the mid-1790s, particularly in mid-Atlantic and New England towns and cities.[36] No less striking than the overlap of biblical and secular arguments was the prevalent conviction that French attacks on Christianity should be understood as a transitory stage on the path to unadulterated Protestantism. As late as 1795 Jedidiah Morse, the geographer and defender of Calvinist orthodoxy who presided over the First Congregational Church in Charlestown, Massachusetts, affirmed confidently that France would eventually turn to Protestantism. Samuel Stillman, a Boston Baptist and Federalist, reassured Christians that France's revolutionary calendar would at least "obliterate . . . every idea of saints days, feasts and fasts, &c. which make a great part of the superstition of the Romish Church."[37] The important point, millennialists insisted, was the lethal blow inflicted upon Catholicism. By sweeping away the most dangerous corruptions of Christianity, the French were preparing the way for the conversion of the Jews and the prophetic triumph of pure religion. It was hardly fortuitous, many millennialists noted, that the British showed their true colors by siding with the Pope. In whatever light American Protestants might view Napoleon, the French seizure of Pope Pius VI in 1798 seemed to mark the end of days for the Beast of Rome.[38]

Although Christian millennialists deplored the violence of the French Revolution, they thought they were witnesses to a fateful struggle between the children of light and the children of darkness, a struggle that had no place for the squeamish. Large numbers of American clergymen defended the French regicides and agreed essentially with Jefferson's statements that "we are not to expect to be translated from despotism to liberty, in a feather-bed," and that "the tree of liberty must be refreshed from time to time with the blood of patriots and tyrants. It is it's natural manure." According to the Western Baptist Morgan John Rhees, whose views on this point were shared by Yale's Congregationalist president Ezra Stiles, the "excesses" of the Terror would not prevent the French Revolution from spreading "the perfect law of liberty" through the entire world.[39] Jefferson himself revealed an apocalyptic mentality in his famous letter rebuking his protégé William Short for criticizing the Jacobins. Sounding more like Thomas Münster, the sixteenth-century radical Anabaptist, than an eighteenth-century defender of inalienable rights, Jefferson asserted that "the liberty of the whole earth was depending on the issue of the contest, and was ever such a prize won with so little innocent blood? My own affections have been deeply wounded by some of the martyrs of this cause, but rather than it should have failed I would have seen half the earth desolated; were there but an Adam and an Eve left in every country, and left free, it would be better than as it now is."[40]

Aside from such an appalling justification for exterminating the innocent in order to perfect the world, Jefferson clearly knew that even Robespierre was no Münster with respect to the rights of property. For the Jacobins, Isser Woloch points out, "equality was a moral and civic concept, which denoted a spirit rather than a condition. Its basic requirements were a popular, responsive government, and social institutions that minimized the consequences of existing inequality and advantages."[41] American Republicans subscribed to a very similar view and could easily endorse the Jacobins' ideal of universal public education and encouragement of widespread property ownership. Even Federalists should have been reassured by Robespierre's proclamation that "equality of wealth is a chimera, necessary neither to private happiness nor to the public welfare," and by the Jacobins' bitter repudiation, after the Thermidorean reaction, of Babeuf's demands for a "genuine equality" based on the abolition of private property. Indeed, conservatives in America and elsewhere might well have learned a lesson about the long-range dangers of martyrdom if they had contemplated the Directory's mistake in 1796 in providing Babeuf and his fellow conspirators with the publicity of a prolonged trial. Yet the very existence of a Conspiracy of Equals, followed by the revival of neo-Jacobinism and the Directory's aggressive support of revolutionary movements from Egypt to Ireland and the Caribbean, aroused increasing alarm in the United States.[42] In a reversal of the earlier confident metaphor, it was now sparks from a panic-stricken England that kindled a counterrevolutionary flame in America.

Much has been written about the political and religious hysteria of the late 1790s, in part because the Alien and Sedition Acts and the accompanying rhetoric of countersubversion anticipated later outbursts of what Richard Hofstadter labeled "the paranoid style," an unfortunate term that I and other historians soon employed.[43] A thorough analysis of this eruption of Francophobia would need to consider many factors, such as the Girondists' naive expectation that the United States would eagerly join the republican crusade to liberate Europe from monarchic despotism; the growing French bitterness over America's disregard for treaty obligations and adoption of a neutrality policy that favored Britain; the arrogant stupidity of the Directory in its handling of the so-called XYZ Affair and provocation of an undeclared naval war with the United States; and the eventual success of Federalist politicians in persuading the clergy, especially in New England, that the Whiskey Rebellion in the West and the activities of the Democratic-Republican societies in the East were part of a French plot to subvert Christianity, private property, and constitutional government.

What interests me here, however, can best be described as a profound paradigm shift with respect to the revolutionary sources of evil. Millennialism, in both its biblical and secular forms, had helped to neutralize traditional fears that power inevitably corrupts and enslaves when unchecked by opposing interests. Foreknowledge of global emancipation allowed millennialists to accept even the most arbitrary and regrettable acts of violence as long as the identity of the forces of evil remained as self-evident as the rights of man. By its very nature, however, millennialism is as reversible as light and darkness or heaven and hell. As the source of evil is redefined, deceptive signs of hope may suddenly signify a long night of premillennial suffering and terror. A joyful sense of new possibilities may actually liberate the world to become enslaved; a spiraling ascent toward the messianic age may prove to be a descent to the holocaust; the Savior may turn out to be the Antichrist.

By 1795 such suspicions had begun to fester among many of New England's clerical leaders as they contemplated the triumph of a Revolutionary Tribunal in Geneva and the arrival of a French army in Holland. It was one thing to subvert the Catholic Church in France and quite another to revolutionize the bastions of European Protestantism. As the Reverend David Osgood mourned in 1795: "Geneva is lost without resource, in respect to religion, to morals, to the fine arts, to trade, to liberty, and above all, to internal peace."[44] Osgood, David Tappan, and Timothy Dwight, the new president of Yale, were even more troubled by signs of domestic danger, such as the popularity of Thomas Paine's *Age of Reason* and other deist works, reports of growing religious infidelity in the West, and the rapid spread of Freemasonry, which directly challenged the clerical Standing Order in Connecticut and other states. When European historians emphasize the relative conservatism that followed the Thermidorean reaction, they often forget that for the English and Americans it was the Directory that appeared to be revolutionizing the world. After Fructidor, French democrats carefully avoided endorsing Babeuf's eccentric ideas but publicized the injustice or "assassination" of the Vendôme trial. American Federalists could easily assert and may even have believed that the true goals of the French Revolution had always been to destroy property, marriage, female modesty, morality, belief in the hereafter, and all "ALTARS OF GOD."[45]

This fantasy was given coherence by the supposed revelations of a former Jesuit, the Abbé Barruel, and a former Scottish Freemason, John Robison. It was Robison, in particular, who popularized the theory that a secret Bavarian Order of the Illuminati had first infiltrated the Freemasonic Order and had then engineered the French Revolution as a way of arousing popular hopes and discontents, overturning established governments, subverting religion, and then, as David Tappan put it, forcing people "at the point of the bayonet, to accept the offered boon of liberty and equality!" The Illuminati combined the secular rationalism of the left-wing Enlightenment with all the diabolical traits once ascribed to the Catholic Counter-Reformation. As Jedidiah Morse and other alarmists suggested, the French Illuminati and their disciples were almost perfectly designed as the Great American Enemy. The conspiratorial brotherhood, as the modernized Antichrist, was highly skilled at using all the means of public influence—glittering egalitarian rhetoric, lists of abuses and grievances, networks of democratic clubs—in order to achieve absolute power and dominion. In fact, in a concave mirror a true Tory might see reflections of the Declaration of Independence and the Sons of Liberty.[46] "Have I not been employed in mischief all my days?" John Adams nervously asked in 1811. "Did not the American Revolution produce the French Revolution? And did not the French Revolution produce all the calamities and desolations to the human race and the whole globe ever since? I meant well, however. . . . I was borne along by an irresistible sense of duty."[47]

When American blacks viewed the mirror's reflections, even the promises of Adams' original revolution seemed to be devices to ensure the absolute power and dominion of whites, whose equality depended in some paradoxical way on the permanent degradation of African-Americans. Even the most ardent white egalitarians had not envisioned a multiracial millennium. Yet Jesus had expressed an ancient millennialist ideal in his parable of the vineyard and warning that "the last shall be first, and the first last." Before being tried and executed in 1831 for leading a slave revolt that killed some sixty whites, Nat Turner said that the Spirit had told him that "the time was fast approaching when the first should be last and the last should be first."[48] For many American whites in the early 1790s this was the terrifying message brought by thousands of refugees, many of them emaciated and in a state of shock, as they streamed into Charleston, Norfolk, Philadelphia, and other port cities from the once fabulously rich French colony of Saint Domingue.

There can be no doubt that this decidedly nonbourgeois revolution, symbolized by numerous tales of white colonists being raped, impaled, and slaughtered by rebellious slaves, stiffened Southern resistance to even cautious proposals for gradual emancipation.[49] Nevertheless, when one considers that an armada of 137 French vessels transported Dominguan refugees to Eastern ports in America soon after Edmond Genet arrived in Philadelphia, it is astonishing that the black Jacobins of the Caribbean did not have more effect on the white public's enthusiasm for the French Revolution.

Certainly many white Americans recoiled in horror when faced with this spectacle of a racial revolution which the armies of France, Spain, and England were unable to suppress. In response to urgent French appeals, the Washington administration authorized modest amounts of emergency aid to prevent the free colonists from starving or being annihilated.[50] Yet American whites were by no means unanimous in condemning the blacks. Abraham Bishop, a Yale classmate in the 1770s of Joel Barlow and Noah Webster, pointed out in December 1791 that the Dominguan slaves were fighting for the same principles Americans had consecrated in their own revolution. Bishop, writing under a pseudonym in a Boston newspaper, mocked the hypocrisy of his countrymen who celebrated the bravery of American rebels who had killed Englishmen but were now shocked when blacks asserted "those rights by the sword which it was impossible to secure by mild measures. —Stripes, imprisonment, hunger, nakedness, cruel tortures and death, were the portion of those Blacks who even talked of liberty, or who, for a moment, conducted like Freemen." Bishop remarked that the American revolutionaries who had taught the world to echo the cry "Liberty or Death!" did not say "all *white* men are *free,* but *all men* are free." The same God who led the Americans to victory, he wrote, "is teaching them, as he taught you, that freedom from the tyranny of men is to be had *only* at the price of blood." Bishop sadly concluded that "from us the blacks had a right to expect effectual assistance. They are pursuing the principles which we had taught them, and are now sealing with their blood, *the rights of men:* yet Americans are sending assistance to their enemies."[51]

Abraham Bishop became a fervent Jeffersonian Republican who in 1802 ridiculed the anti-Illuminati hysteria by accusing the Federalists themselves of plotting to overthrow popular liberty and the true spirit of Christianity. Yet Theodore Dwight, a no less dedicated Federalist, a grandson of Jonathan Edwards and brother of the ultraconservative Timothy Dwight, was no less radical than Bishop in his support for the Dominguan black rebels. And Dwight spoke in the spring of 1794, at the height of the French Reign of Terror and at a time when British troops were fighting to reimpose slavery in Saint Domingue. In a speech to Connecticut's Society for the Promotion of Freedom and the Relief of Persons Unlawfully Holden in Bondage, Dwight, a lawyer, took the uncompromising position that slaves had been illegally deprived of such "absolute rights" as personal security and personal liberty. Since they had been brought into New World societies by force and were not parties to the social compact, he reasoned, they were not subject to any customs or laws, "unless designed as a partial compensation for the injuries which they have suffered—injuries, for which all the wealth of man can never atone."[52]

For Dwight it followed that any law sanctioning defensive war "will justify slaves for every necessary act of defence, against the wicked, and unprovoked outrages, committed against their peace, freedom, and existence." In other words, slaves owed neither obedience nor gratitude to the laws that ruled them. In Saint Domingue a "succession of unjust, and contradictory measures" had finally "exasperated the negroes, and roused their spirits to unanimity and fanaticism. Seized by the phrenzy of oppressed human nature, they suddenly awoke from the lethargy of slavery, attacked their tyrannical masters, spread desolation and blood over the face of the colony, and by a series of vigorous efforts, established themselves on the firm pillars of freedom and independence."

Since the whites in France had not been released from the obligations of the social compact, Dwight had no tolerance for what he called the "profligate, and blood-thirsty junto" that had seized control of the French Revolution and "forced the infatuated republic to assassination and ruin." But, like various other antislavery spokesmen of the early and mid-1790s, he hoped that the events in Saint Domingue would teach Southerners that the scenes of bloody retribution described by the prophet Jeremiah were "the natural, and necessary consequences of slavery, in every country, where the slaves are more numerous than their masters." It was up to Southern slaveholders to begin eradicating an evil that would otherwise destroy them. Once the slaves revolted, Dwight warned, their masters should expect no aid from any friend of freedom and justice. He said nothing about offering refuge to escaped or self-liberated blacks.[53]

Among American whites, Bishop and Dwight were clearly exceptional. And such bold outbursts waned along with the more general enthusiasm for the French Revolution. For blacks, however, the Haitian Revolution took on symbolic meanings that endured at least in covert oral tradition. Fragmentary evidence suggests that Gabriel Prosser's massive slave conspiracy of 1800 in Virginia, like similar conspiracies and insurrections in Venezuela, Cuba, Louisiana, and Barbados, was partly inspired by knowledge of the slaves' success in Saint Domingue. It is true that slave revolts were not as common after 1804 as in the eighteenth century. There can be no doubt, however, that Denmark Vesey, the free black leader of the momentous 1822 slave conspiracy in Charleston, took a lively interest in the Haitian Revolution. In the trials following the exposure of the plot, one rebel testified that Vesey "was in the habit of reading to me all the passages in the newspapers that related to St. Domingo, and apparently every pamphlet he could lay his hands on that had any connection with slavery." Other slave testimony referred to letters sent to Haiti requesting aid and to one of Vesey's followers' promising "that St. Domingo and Africa would come over and cut up the white people if we only made the motion here first." The evidence suggests that Vesey may have hoped to gain assistance from Haiti and the North and to sail to Haiti after exterminating the whites and destroying Charleston. Henry William Desaussure, South Carolina's leading jurist, spoke of the rebels' appealing to the Haitians "as their natural allies." Predictably he used the history of Haiti as an example of the destructive civil wars that would inevitably follow any move toward slave emancipation.[54]

While the Haitian example inspired a number of violent conspiracies and revolts, it had a deeper and more lasting impact on the self-image and nascent national identity of free blacks, especially in the northern United States. What impressed black leaders like James Forten, a prosperous sailmaker and entrepreneur in Philadelphia, was not the violence that could be attributed to war and to slavery itself. It was rather the providential message that the black people "would become a great nation" and "could not always be detained in their present bondage." By the 1820s, when John Russwurm in a commencement address at Bowdoin College eulogized the Haitian patriots as the black equivalents of the Founding Fathers, and when blacks in various cities began celebrating the anniversary of Haitian independence, the revolution became a symbolic negation of everything slavery represented. As one speaker in Baltimore put it, Haiti had become "an irrefutable argument to prove . . . that the descendants of Africa never were designed by their Creator to sustain an inferiority, or even a mediocrity, in the chain of being; but they are as capable of intellectual improvement as Europeans, or any other nation upon the face of the earth." David Walker, in his revolutionary *Appeal to the Coloured Citizens of the World*, urged his brethren to read the history of Haiti, which he termed "the glory of the blacks and terror of tyrants." [55]

So the French Revolution, which included the liberation of Haiti, had profound and continuing reverberations in the United States. The emancipation of slaves in Haiti and in many of the newly independent Hispanic American republics, whose wars with Spain were ignited by Europe's revolutionary upheavals, tested the revolutionary self-image of the United States. [56] No doubt the poverty and political instability of the Haitian and Hispanic American republics provided ammunition for North American racists and defenders of slavery. But invidious comparisons and patriotic self-satisfaction could only partly conceal the nation's anxieties over the unforeseeable consequences of revolutionary influence.

III

THE
STRUGGLE
TO PRESERVE A
REVOLUTIONARY
AMERICA

✺

I N 1824 HENRY DWIGHT SEDGWICK felt compelled to confront the specter of the French Revolution in a cautious and reasoned essay on legal reform. The editors of the staid *North American Review* had chosen Sedgwick, the author of a treatise on common law and the son of the crusty Federalist senator and judge, Theodore Sedgwick, to review William Sampson's slashing attack on English jurisprudence. Since the elder Judge Sedgwick had referred to the common people as Jacobins and sansculottes, it seemed unlikely that his son would be sympathetic to Sampson, a radical attorney and Irish Catholic who had been deported from England and had then won notoriety for his defense of unionized journeymen cordwainers in a famous conspiracy trial in New York City. But although Henry Sedgwick expressed perfunctory respect for the common law's devotion to freedom, he used his review of Sampson as a means of advocating written codes designed to meet new needs and conditions and of criticizing what he termed an "excessive veneration for authority [that] binds one age in the chains of another."

As a defender of innovation and progress, Sedgwick anticipated his critics by acknowledging that the French Revolution had been "the most tremendous innovation which ever convulsed the established order of things." But the fires of this "moral Vesuvius," he continued, are already extinct, "and its desolating lava has mingled with and fertilized the soil." In any event, Sedgwick boldly asked, what were the costs of the French Revolution "compared with the unvarying despotism, and the changeless castes of the East, where every effort of the intellect, and every impulse of the heart, is repressed not less by the tyranny of custom, and ancient and venerated usage, than by the sword of power?" From an objective, long-term perspective, there had been "comparatively few victims" of revolutionary innovations; yet "disregarded millions," Sedgwick pointed out, "have pined and perished under the chains of habit, prejudice, and authority." Unfortunately, he added, the highly publicized mistakes and violence occasioned by revolution had aroused alarm and prolonged prejudice against all forms of human improvement among people who never considered the costs of less dramatic forms of oppression, such as "the tyranny of the Aristotelian system."[1]

Nearly twenty years later the aging abolitionist William Goodell gave the French Revolution a central place in explaining "the marked decline of the spirit of liberty in this country for half a century after the [American] Revolution." A devout and orthodox Christian, Goodell had served as a merchant seaman on voyages to the East Indies, China, and Europe before turning to temperance reform, abolitionism, and attacks on racial prejudice and what he termed "the aristocracy of wealth." He believed that the "excesses" of the French Revolution, "commencing soon after our Federal Government went into operation, must have contributed largely, as we know it did, to bring democratic principles into disrepute, to increase and fortify the jealousies and fears of [conservatives], and confirm the impression of insecurity to life, to property, and to civil order, if large masses of men should at once be released from absolute control."

As an abolitionist, Goodell had repeatedly heard the objection that, "if millions of educated and polished Frenchmen could not be transferred at once from a state of mere political servility to a state of civil and political freedom, without becoming fired with the frenzy of demons," what could one expect from a far more degraded and ignorant population of slaves? Defenders of slavery had only to point to what Goodell called "the perverted story of 'the horrors of St. Domingo.'" He recalled that at "the beginnings of the present anti-slavery agitation, in 1833, the 'reign of terror' in France, and 'the horrors of St. Domingo,' were successfully adverted to by opposers; and the doctrines of immediate and unconditional emancipation, as taught by [Jonathan] Edwards [the younger], were systematically confounded with the 'Jacobinism of the first French Revolution'—a misrepresentation less excusable now, than during the dimness and confusion near the close of the last century."[2]

These random examples, representing two quite different kinds of advocacy, suggest the depth and persistence of the counterrevolutionary phobia that nineteenth-century American reformers were forced to overcome. While some might object that Sedgwick and Goodell were addressing mainly northeastern ex-Federalist or Whiggish audiences, Goodell made it clear that defenders of slavery in the South had appropriated and transmuted the stock Francophobe arguments. If racial slavery had become what James Henry Hammond termed the "very mud-sill of society," traditional Federalist fears of democracy could easily be translated into an open and unashamed denial of human equality by leaders who nevertheless affirmed the equality of the white master race. As early as 1820 John Quincy Adams was shocked to hear John C. Calhoun maintain, as they walked home together after conferring with President Monroe about the Missouri Compromise, that to limit "degrading" labor to slaves "was the best guarantee to equality among whites. It produced an unvarying level among them. It not only did not excite, but did not even admit of inequalities, by which one white man could domineer over another." When Georgia's Governor Joseph E. Brown campaigned for disunion after the election of 1860, warning his state's nonslaveholding northern uplands that the new Republican government would enable mobs of emancipated blacks to move into the healthier valleys to plunder and kill, he assured the legislature that "slavery is the poor man's best Government," since "among us the poor white laborer is respected as an equal. His family is treated with kindness, consideration, and respect. He does not belong to the menial class. The negro is in no sense his equal. . . . He belongs to the only true aristocracy, the race of *white men*."[3]

Speaking of the early nineteenth century, Goodell contended that the French Revolution had made it easier for the Federalists to keep their theory of civil government from becoming more democratic and had also allowed the Democratic-Republicans to refrain from reducing their theories to practice. In consequence, Americans had betrayed the principles of their own Revolution even as they joined together in celebrating it as a unifying ritual. As Abraham Lincoln bitterly wrote in 1855, after observing how the greed to become masters of slaves had led many Americans to dismiss equality as "a self-evident lie," "the fourth of July has not quite dwindled away; it is still a great day—*for burning fire-crackers!!!*"[4]

It would be a serious mistake, however, to conclude that reactions against the French Revolution negated the desire of Americans to extend and fulfill the promise of their own Revolution. Sedgwick's reappraisal of the French Revolution appeared during Lafayette's "triumphal tour" of the United States in 1824–25, which multitudes of Americans viewed as the republican equivalent of the Second Coming. Hailed as Washington's adopted "apostle of liberty" and as the embodiment of disinterested benevolence, Lafayette had first aided America in its struggle for independence and had then become, according to the prevailing mythology, the only true hero of the French Revolution. After transmitting American republican principles back to France, he had resisted every temptation to seize power, had resigned his command of the National Guards, and had risked death by consistently supporting the Constitution of 1791 and later declining offices offered by Bonaparte. To cap this record, Lafayette was the only Founding Father who could return to the United States after an absence of forty years in the wilderness and judge the success of the original Revolutionary experiment. If his extensive tour encouraged nationalistic kitch and self-congratulation, it also evoked anxious self-examination and calls for a recovery of sacred Revolutionary principles that had been corroded by greed, hypocrisy, and betrayal. American reformers, including black and white abolitionists, repeatedly wrote to Lafayette seeking his sanction.[5]

Both Goodell and Sedgwick illustrate the determination of reformers of all kinds to revivify the Spirit of '76 and keep America revolutionary by applying the principles of the Declaration of Independence to newly discovered "abuses and usurpations" leading toward tyranny and despotism. In the late 1820s Working Men's parties in Philadelphia and New York submitted lists of facts to a candid world that in effect proved "a history of repeated injuries and usurpations" that threatened to deprive workingmen of their natural rights while favoring monopoly and exclusive privilege. To deprive men of the fruits of their labor or to exclude them from owning property, especially their "birth-right in the soil," was to deprive them of life, liberty, and the pursuit of happiness.[6] In 1830 the anti-Masonic movement issued its own Anti-Masonic Declaration of Independence, accusing the secret Freemason Order of numerous crimes and abuses, including the destruction of "all principles of equality, by bestowing favors on its own members, to the exclusion of others equally meritorious and deserving."[7]

In the famous Declaration of Sentiments of 1848, adopted by the first women's rights convention in human history, feminists extended the principles of the American Revolution to the entire "history of mankind": "a history of repeated injuries and usurpations on the part of man toward woman, having in direct object the establishment of an absolute tyranny over her."[8] This list of grievances, long the butt of male ridicule, now seems more radical and conceptually innovative than Jefferson's original "assemblage of horrors" or even the declarations proclaimed during Europe's contemporary Revolution of 1848.

In 1833 the Declaration of the National Anti-Slavery Convention specifically repudiated the idea that appeals to America's Revolutionary tradition precluded a transcendence of that tradition. In other words, abolitionists could be inspired by the courage and dedication of the Founders and yet vow to go far beyond them in completing what they had left incomplete, in achieving a goal that "for its magnitude, solemnity, and probable results upon the destiny of the world, as far transcends theirs, as moral truth does physical force." For the Founding Fathers' grievances, "great as they were, were trifling in comparison with the wrongs and sufferings of those for whom we plead. Our fathers were never slaves—never bought and sold like cattle—never shut out from the light of knowledge and religion—never subjected to the lash of brutal taskmasters."[9] David Walker and other free blacks had earlier said much the same thing. After quoting extensively from the Declaration of Independence, Walker in 1829 had asked American whites whether they understood their own language: "I ask you candidly, was your sufferings under Great Britain, one hundredth part as cruel and tyranical as you have rendered ours under you?" More than a generation later, at the beginning of Reconstruction, Southern black conventions repeatedly referred to the Declaration as their fundamental and sacred text. As the historian Eric Foner writes, "eleven Alabama blacks, who complained of contract frauds, injustice before the courts, and other abuses, concluded their petition with a revealing masterpiece of understatement: 'This is not the persuit of happiness.'"[10]

In marked contrast to the French, who have remained sharply divided for and against their Revolution throughout the nineteenth and much of the twentieth centuries, Americans found a common source of justification and higher law in their own Revolutionary heritage.[11] Obviously, this sacred precedent had very different meanings for Frederick Douglass and John C. Calhoun, for Jefferson Davis and Abraham Lincoln. Even by 1850, according to Calhoun, the North's numerical majority had converted what was once "a constitutional federal republic" into a system "as absolute as that of the Autocrat of Russia, and as despotic in its tendency as any absolute government that ever existed." A decade later the South self-consciously followed the precedent of the American Revolution when it proclaimed its independence and framed a "purified" constitution for confederated self-government. But for Lincoln, brooding in 1855 over the spread of slavery and anti-immigrant Know Nothingism, the nation had degenerated from its Revolutionary principles in an altogether different way: "As a nation, we began by declaring that '*all men are created equal.*' We now practically read it 'all men are created equal, *except negroes.*' When the Know-Nothings get control, it will read 'all men are created equal, except negroes, *and foreigners, and catholics.*' When it comes to this I should prefer emigrating to some country where they make no pretence of loving liberty— to Russia, for instance, where despotism can be taken pure, and without the base alloy of hypocracy."[12]

Lincoln and Calhoun could at least agree that America's Revolutionary tradition, though corrupted in their own day, should make the United States the antithesis of czarist Russia. Lincoln was willing to sacrifice hundreds of thousands of lives, in "a new birth of freedom," to prove that a nation dedicated to the proposition that all men are created equal "can long endure." One result of the Civil War for many Unionists was to qualify if not undermine belief in the inherent right of revolution and to idealize loyalty to the nation-state. To some degree the loyalty oaths demanded by Lincoln and Andrew Johnson became substitutes for "the consent of the governed."

From this standpoint, the difference between the American and French revolutionary traditions is especially remarkable in view of the canonization of Thomas Jefferson, once an apologist for the French Reign of Terror, as the spokesman and interpreter of the American republican cause.[13] Writing to Jefferson in 1813, John Adams attributed his own "immense Unpopularity" to his frank forebodings that the French Revolution would lead to disaster; yet, according to Adams, Jefferson's "steady defence of democratical Principles, and your invariable favourable Opinion of the french Revolution laid the foundation of your Unbounded Popularity." Certainly Jefferson had not ruined his image by writing that "I hold it that a little rebellion now and then is a good thing, and as necessary in the political world as storms in the physical." Or, in lines that deserve to be immortalized in all human societies and that continue to acquire new relevance, "And what country can preserve it's liberties if their rulers are not warned from time to time that their people preserve the spirit of resistance?"[14]

With respect to the French Revolution, however, Jefferson eventually veered some distance toward the judgment of his old friend and political rival John Adams. The famous correspondence between the two retired presidents contains some of the richest reflections we have on the course of modern history as well as two sets of assumptions, both grounded in the American Revolutionary experience, that would long influence American responses to foreign movements for liberation. Writing in 1811 to his friend Benjamin Rush, who was encouraging a reconciliation between Adams and Jefferson, Adams claimed that he and Jefferson had never differed on the essential principles of republicanism, on the Constitution, or on the "forms of government in general." Adams' crucial point of departure from both Jefferson and Rush had been his correct understanding that the French Revolution "could end only in a restoration of the Bourbons, or a military despotism, after deluging France and Europe in blood." He assured Rush that he had never regarded Jefferson as an enemy and believed "you both to mean well to mankind and your country," even if "perhaps unconsciously . . . [your opinions were] a little swayed by a love of popularity and possibly by a little spice of ambition." [15] For all his cordiality, Adams still smarted from accusations of being a monarchist in disguise and a traitor to the republican cause. Obsessed with his unpopularity, he longed for vindication.

It was all very well, Adams thought, for Jefferson to philosophize at his rural retreat surrounded by black servants. [16] But Jefferson had never felt what Adams called "the Terrorism" of Shays's Rebellion, the Whiskey Rebellion, and Fries Rebellion. "You certainly never felt the Terrorism," Adams wrote in 1813, "excited by Genet, in 1793, when ten thousand People in the Streets of Philadelphia, day after day, threatened to drag Washington out of his House, and effect a Revolution in the Government, or compel it to declare War in favour of the French Revolution, and against England." In 1799, when Adams as president had proclaimed a fast day to protect the nation against disunion, sedition, and insurrection, he claimed that a mob of thousands had besieged his house in Philadelphia. "Determined to defend my House at the Expence of my Life, and the Lives of the few, very few Domesticks and Friends within it," Adams wrote, he had ordered chests of arms from the War Office "to be brought through bye Lanes and back Doors." Recalling the names of culpable Republican journalists and agitators, offering now to give anything for a complete collection of the circular letters sent by Congressmen to their constituents in the middle and southern states, Adams asked, "What think you of Terrorism, Mr. Jefferson?" [17] One can only wonder whether Adams was tempted to mention the terrorism of the Haitian Revolution or Gabriel's massive slave conspiracy to capture Richmond. His total silence on this score is not insignificant, especially in view of his later admission to Jefferson that "Slavery in this Country I have seen hanging over it like a black cloud for half a Century."[18]

In any event, Adams was immensely pleased and consoled to receive a letter early in 1816 in which Jefferson fully agreed with his "eulogies on the 18th. century," an age when "the sciences and arts, manners and morals, advanced to a higher degree than the world had ever before seen." Adams had long maintained that when he had lived in Europe, from 1778 to 1785, the nations appeared "to be advancing by slow but sure Steps towards an Amelioration of the condition of Man, in Religion and Government, in Liberty, Equality, Fraternity Knowledge Civilization and Humanity." The French Revolution had then put the continent on "a retrograde course, for at least a Century, if not many Centuries."[19] Jefferson now agreed that "the close of the century saw the moral world thrown back again to the age of the Borgias, to the point from which it had departed 300. years before." He carefully refrained from specifying the French Revolution as the source of this calamity, though to Lafayette he had earlier affirmed that French republicans had committed a "fatal error" in not stopping with a "limited monarchy," as Lafayette had wished to do, in order to avoid the "unprincipled and bloody tyranny" of Robespierre and Bonaparte.[20] To Adams he mentioned the prerevolutionary "atrocity" of Poland's partition and the counterrevolutionary Treaty of Pilnitz, acts which unblushingly established the principle "that power was right." He referred to "the terror of monarchs, alarmed at the light returning on them from the West, and kindling a Volcano under their thrones." But Jefferson also acknowledged that "France, after crushing and punishing the conspiracy of Pilnitz, went herself deeper and deeper into the crimes she had been chastising. I say France, and not Bonaparte; for altho' he was the head and mouth, the nation furnished the hands which executed his enormities. England, altho' in opposition, kept full pace with France, not indeed by the manly force of her own arms, but by oppressing the weak, and bribing the strong."[21]

Jefferson freely admitted that Adams' early prophecies to Richard Price had "proved truer than mine." Indeed, while Adams had been quoted as predicting a million deaths, Jefferson now estimated that between eight and ten million human beings had been killed as a result "of these convulsions." For Jefferson, however, the story was far from being complete and the retrogression or backward spiral of the French Revolution gave no reason to abandon hope in the inevitability of historical progress. "The same light from our West" that had terrorized Europe's monarchs, he assured Adams, "seems to have spread and illuminated the very engines employed to extinguish it." Since the idea of representative government had taken root among the people, their masters were already trying to save themselves "by timely offers of this modification of their own powers." No doubt reforms would be illusory at first; "rivers of blood may yet flow"; but "even France," Jefferson affirmed, "will yet attain representative government." What were the grounds for such confidence when Jefferson himself foresaw Europe again becoming "an Arena of gladiators"? Apart from what he later called his sanguine temperament, Jefferson's hopes stemmed from his conviction, presumably confirmed by the American Revolution he and Adams had helped to lead, that "opinion is power, and that opinion will come."[22]

Because of the growing warmth and cordiality of their correspondence, Jefferson and Adams appeared to be as close to agreement on foreign revolutions as on the attributes of a natural aristocracy, the Catholic and even Protestant corruptions of Christianity, and the primacy of education and diffusing knowledge. Adams, for example, concurred with Jefferson's speculations concerning the future of Europe, adding only a cautionary warning that progress would be slow since so many forces obstructed or discouraged the dissemination of knowledge. One is easily misled, however, by the friendship and consensus of two former presidents who had led the most bitterly partisan factions before the Civil War and who prefigured in many respects the conflicting responses of the United States to future revolutions.

Adams was essentially a devout monotheist who detested the idolatry and self-aggrandizement of priests, preachers, philosophers, and political saviors who paraded beyond the austere boundaries established by the Ten Commandments and the Sermon on the Mount. Human reason and conscience, he wrote Jefferson, "are not a Match for human Passions, human Imaginations and human Enthusiasm."[23] The more Adams studied history and philosophy, the more impressed he became by the human capacity for self-deception and the corrupting allure and effects of power. "Power," he wrote in 1816, "always thinks it has a great Soul, and vast Views, beyond the Comprehension of the Weak; and that it is doing God Service, when it is violating all his Laws." These indubitable but often forgotten truths led Adams to such maxims as "Power must never be trusted without a Check," and "Britain will never be our Friend, till We are her Master. . . . I am well assured that nothing will restrain G.B. from injuring Us, but fear."[24]

For Adams these traditional doctrines of the American Revolution were inseparably tied to a profound antipathy toward all forms of millennialism, sacred and secular. He recalled his utter amazement at hearing Dr. Joseph Priestley assert, soon after the execution of Louix XVI, that the French Revolution "was opening a new era in the world and presenting a near view of the millenium." Since Adams and Priestley were having breakfast in private, Adams pressed the learned scientist whether he had ever encountered evidence in ancient or modern history that "such multitudes of ignorant people ever were or ever can be converted suddenly into materials capable of conducting a free government especially a democratical republic?" Priestley, after acknowledging that he knew of no such evidence, finally admitted that "my opinion is founded altogether upon revelation and the prophecies; I take it that the ten horns of the great beast in revelations, mean the ten crowned heads of Europe: and that the execution of the king of France is the falling off of the first of those horns." Such was "the enthusiasm," as Adams puts it, "of that great man, that reasoning machine."[25]

Messianic enthusiasm, Adams well knew, was not confined to biblicists or even believers in God. Like the twentieth-century historian Carl Becker, he concluded that the eighteenth-century philosophers had created their own Heavenly City and their own version of the ancient priestly principle that "When it is to combat Evil, 'tis lawful to employ the Devil." For a skeptical Yankee, whose "Spirit of Prophecy reaches no farther than, *New England* GUESSES," there was thus a sinister kinship between the Crusades, the Inquisition, and the French Revolution.[26] This did not mean that Adams rejected belief in social improvement or in moving toward a system that would prove more successful in identifying and rewarding virtue and talent, the marks of natural aristocracy that could be found, he emphasized, among women as well as men and among all classes of society.[27] But for him true progress was continuous, gradual, and cumulative. He was immediately suspicious of apocalyptic moments and eschatological judgments; one can almost feel Adams shudder when Jefferson continued to talk cavalierly about attaining goals that were "worth rivers of blood, and years of desolation."[28]

Since Jefferson and Adams were constantly seeking points

of agreement as they contemplated the follies of the post-Napoleonic world, their differences seemed largely a matter of emphasis. They knew that occasions arise when only violence or the threat of violence could dislodge and remedy deeply entrenched injustice. They had also learned that power exercised for such seemingly righteous ends could destroy liberty and produce new and hideous forms of inequality. Yet only Jefferson could have written: "I steer my bark with Hope in the head, leaving Fear astern. My hopes indeed sometimes fail; but not oftener than the forebodings of the gloomy."[29] Jefferson and his later disciples could greet each new revolution with hope, as the dawn of a new era, precisely because they knew with the certainty of ancient prophets that God's cause, the cause of freedom and virtue, would eventually prevail.

It is true that in 1823, when Jefferson was discouraged by the outcome of the Latin American wars of independence and the suppression of democratic movements in Spain, Piedmont, and Naples, he concurred with Adams' views on the difficulties of overthrowing despotism. "The generation which commences a revolution" he wrote, "can rarely compleat it." Though Jefferson did not allude to the Bible, his reasoning echoed the explanation given for the failure of Moses and the first generation in the Israelite Exodus to reach the Promised Land. Most revolutionaries, Jefferson pointed out, "habituated from their infancy to passive submission of body and mind to their kings and priests," were simply not qualified to think for themselves, assume the responsibilities of freedom, and guard against the plots of would-be Napoleons to take over a revolution for their own selfish ends. Ironically, Jefferson's theory implied that the only people truly prepared for a successful revolution were those who had been the least oppressed—a people already trained in representative government, freed from religious authority, committed to a free press and habeas corpus, familiar with "a qualified negative on their laws," and enlightened by the practical experience of jury trials.[30] It is all too easy to satirize such a list of republican entrance requirements and conclude that America's apostle of liberty now wished to confine revolutions to people like Adams and himself. But in the same letter of 1821 in which Jefferson expressed his fear that the Hispanic Americans were not yet prepared for self-government and would end up with "military tyrannies," he "wished them success" in their experiment and predicted that it would only be a matter of time before they learned the habits of freedom, self-improvement, and self-government that would enable them "to break entirely from the parent stem." Moreover, having referred earlier to the fatal Missouri crisis and possibility of civil war, he ingenuously confided to Adams: "You see, my dear Sir, how easily we prescribe for others a cure for their difficulties, while we cannot cure our own."[31] This note of humility has been conspicuously absent in most of the writings of Jefferson's and Adams's more recent critics.

Despite Jefferson's talk of preparatory knowledge and experience, his faith in revolution was hardly less universalistic than that of Karl Marx. Unlike some imperialists of a later era, he did not think of the extension of liberty, equality, and self-government as the Americanization of the world. Bitterly distrustful of England and what he called the "Northern triumvirate" of Austria, Prussia, and Russia, "arming their nations to dictate despotisms to the rest of the world," he saw the United States as a lone and encircled bastion of liberty. Yet no temporary reverses, not even four or five successive failures, could prevent the spread of the revolutionary flames first kindled in 1776. "In France," according to Jefferson's retrospective diagnosis of 1823, "the 1st effort was defeated by Robespierre, the 2d. by Bonaparte, the 3d. by Louis XVIII. and his holy allies." But the waves of revolt would continue, for, "as a younger, and more instructed race comes on, the sentiment becomes more and more intuitive." "Rivers of blood must yet flow," Jefferson continued, as he imagined Adams and himself looking down from another world as Spain, Portugal, Italy, Prussia, Germany, and Greece all won freedom and representative government, achievements "which will add to the joys even of heaven."[32]

Whatever joys Jefferson experienced in paradise, he may well have beamed eighty-eight years later when William Jennings Bryan, thrilled by the news of a republican revolution in China, shipped an encyclopedia of Jefferson's writings to Yuan Shikai in Beijing, except that in heaven Jefferson would have known that Bryan had chosen the wrong leader to support.[33] One can easily assemble quotations expressing Americans' jubilation or foreboding in response to the European revolutions of 1830 and 1848, the Russian revolutions of 1905 and 1917, the Chinese Revolution of 1911–12, and the Mexican Revolution of 1913–14, to say nothing of the more recent Communist revolutions in China, Cuba, and Vietnam. Often at variance with official United States policy, such responses have reflected the increasing ethnic, class, religious, and ideological diversity of American society as well as the country's commercial, corporate, missionary, and military involvement in other nations and cultures. Bryan's support of the Chinese Revolution, for example, drew on the enthusiasm of missionaries and his own democratic creed, which contradicted the caution of powerful business interests and "old China hands," who tended to believe that republican institutions were "unsuited to the genius of an Oriental people."[34] When considering the contradictory responses of Americans, one should not forget the contradictory and polemical responses of the foreign revolutionaries themselves, who for almost two centuries have been asking, "Who betrayed us?" "What was it that went wrong?" "Why did a Napoleonic dictatorship or *Stalinshchina* emerge in the place of democratic socialism?" Despite such complexity, it is important to identify certain long-term patterns of continuity that often swung from Jefferson's hopeful expectancy to Adams' suspicion of messianic deception or a "goblin damned," before we return briefly to some connections between foreign liberation and American conceptions of equality.

In view of the profound if delayed American reaction against the French and Haitian revolutions, I am struck first of all by the continuing enthusiasm and hopeful expectations with which the press and general public have greeted news of foreign revolutions from the South American struggles of Francisco de Miranda and José Miguel Carrera in 1811 to the tributes lavished on Fidel Castro in 1959 by the *New York Times, Reader's Digest,* the *Christian Science Monitor,* the *New Republic,* and even *Life* and *Look* magazines.[35] Although historians usually have portrayed the United States as a decidedly nonrevolutionary if not counterrevolutionary society, we must at least take account of this remarkable receptivity to the idea of revolution, which has risen and fallen with the regularity and persistence of religious revivals. Indeed, the cycle of declension and rebirth, signaled by a "new era" of revolutionary hope, may well have become the revival's secular analogue for numerous journalists, novelists, reformers, academics, and other intellectuals. Some of these liberal opinion-shapers, such as the privileged Philadelphians Richard Rush and William C. Bullitt, viewed European revolutions while heading American diplomatic missions. The youthful Bullitt, dispatched early in 1919 to make contact with the Bolsheviks, exclaimed to the accompanying journalist Lincoln Steffens, "We have seen the future and it works!" Like Rush, who as America's minister to France in 1848 took it upon himself to accord virtual recognition to the revolutionary Second Republic, Bullitt went beyond his instructions and negotiated an agreement with Lenin that appeared highly favorable for the Allied Powers.

During his brief visit to Russia, Bullitt believed the idealistic rhetoric and exaggerated claims of the Soviet leaders and felt both betrayed and disillusioned when President Wilson and the Allies refused even to consider Lenin's peace proposal. But in 1848 Rush had little need to fear displeasing the British and was heartened that Secretary of State James Buchanan not only approved his action but wrote that "with one universal burst of enthusiasm . . . the American people hailed the late glorious revolution in France in favor of liberty and republican government."[36]

American foreign policy was constrained of course by the ideal of neutrality bequeathed by President Washington, a norm that acquired almost constitutional force. That tradition, together with the legend of Lafayette, obscured the fact that Americans owed their independence to a foreign alliance they had failed to honor, not to a gallant French volunteer. Although a few would-be American Lafayettes aspired to aid the Hispanic Americans, Greeks, French, Poles, and other fighters for freedom, America's relations with the revolutions of the first half of the nineteenth century were complicated by the nation's official commitment to neutrality, by fear of commercial or military retaliation, and by the confusion between democratic revolutions and wars for national independence, typified by the popular adulation of Lajos Kossuth, the exiled Hungarian patriot. Significantly, Kossuth received little acclaim either in the slaveholding South or from abolitionists, who were incensed by his refusal to speak out on the issue of slavery and angered by the opportunity he gave a slaveholding nation to flaunt its dedication to freedom and republican principles.[37] America's role in a revolutionary world was always complicated by what James Madison repeatedly called "the blot" or "the stain" of racial slavery. The Father of the Constitution and America's most original ideologist of republicanism never doubted, in Drew R. McCoy's words, "that the persistence of the peculiar institution significantly impaired the moral force of America's republican example in the rest of the world."[38]

Yet McCoy also emphasizes that Madison and other leading statesmen were convinced that republicanism would eventually overcome both slavery and what Madison termed "the horrors of the Revolutionary experiment in France," the two obstacles that had impeded the overthrow of monarchy and despotism throughout Europe and the Western Hemisphere. Convinced that the American Revolution had inaugurated a new epoch in human history, Madison rejoiced in the belief that the "newborn nations" of Latin America, which had embarked on "the same great experiment of self-government," were "alive to what they owe to our example, as well in the origin of their career as in the forms of their institutions."[39] Henry Clay, the leading champion of the Latin American revolutionaries and critic of the Monroe administration's policy of strict neutrality, went even farther in applauding "the glorious spectacle of eighteen millions of people, struggling to burst their chains and to be free." To the opponents of intervention who portrayed Latin Americans as a degenerate mixed race, ignorant and wholly unprepared for self-government, Clay replied in 1820 that several of the new republics had advanced beyond the United States at least in one respect: they were already emancipating their slaves.[40]

This was an astounding assertion for an ambitious young slaveholding politician to make, even if one acknowledges the widespread hope in the Upper South that both slaves and free blacks were destined to migrate to more congenial climes. For a brief period, however, reports from South America encouraged the belief that anything was possible if the oldest slave systems in the Hemisphere were beginning to collapse. While Clay and others exaggerated the speed and effectiveness of slave emancipation in Hispanic America, the wars of independence had made it necessary to recruit increasing numbers of black and colored troops; as the price of aid from Haiti, Simón Bolívar had promised to emancipate slaves in the Spanish colonies he liberated.[41] Yet after the United States had weathered the Missouri Crisis and the panic over Denmark Vesey's conspiracy, most Southerners were appalled by Clay's enthusiasm, as Secretary of State, for sending delegates to Bolívar's Pan-American Convention of 1826, a conference that was likely to recognize Haiti and applaud the emancipation laws that had by then been enacted by nearly all the Latin American republics.

Apart from the issues of slavery and race, North American views of Latin American revolution had always been entangled with traditional anti-Hispanic prejudices and imperialist designs and intrigues to seize Cuba and Spanish borderland territories. In 1818, when Clay envisioned the United States as the leader of a New World republican system, "a sort of counterpoise of the Holy Alliance," the Monroe administration was preoccupied with the Florida crisis and the crucial Adams-Onís Treaty, which would define the southern and western boundaries of the United States. Nevertheless, in 1816 *Niles' Weekly Register* reported that most of the American people were "heartily devoted to the success of the patriots," and two years later Americans toasted Latin American independence at innumerable Fourth of July celebrations, hailing Clay as "the independent and enlightened statesman, and the eloquent defender of South American liberty and the best interests of our country."[42]

In 1830 there was far less ambiguity and division with respect to Europe. The barricades of July that appeared throughout Paris in unsurpassed numbers were part of a much wider upheaval that included agrarian unrest, machine-destruction, and mass demonstrations in England; an immense Polish insurrection against Russian despotism; rioting in Belgium and the proclamation of Belgian independence; uprisings in

Italy and the launching of Mazzini's revolutionary Young Italy movement, echoed by similar romantic nationalist movements throughout the Germanic Confederation and Austrian Empire.[43] At this moment in history, as Tocqueville and other travelers attested, the United States seemed to have achieved the major goals to which European liberals aspired: wholly freed from kings, nobility, and foreign control, Americans had adopted what was said to be universal manhood suffrage, while nurturing political, religious, and social institutions that preserved liberty and mitigated the tyrannical power of the majority.

For self-satisfied Jacksonian Democrats or slaveholders who welcomed a safe opportunity to cheer for freedom and progress, the revolutions of 1830 marked "the opening of a new era" that would bring Europe closer to the American model. In the words of Henry C. Rives, a liberal-minded slaveholder and colonizationist appointed by President Jackson as America's minister in Paris, the July Days represented "one of the most wonderful revolutions which have ever occurred in the history of the world." Jackson himself in his December message to Congress referred to the "courage and wisdom" of the French people, whose revolution had evoked a "spontaneous and universal burst of applause" from his fellow citizens—a reference perhaps to the recent gathering in Washington of some thirty thousand people to celebrate the establishment in France of Louis Philippe's liberal monarchy, which both Tocqueville and Marx later labeled, from wholly different perspectives, a "joint stock company of the bourgeoisie."[44]

The extraordinary American enthusiasm for the Greeks' long struggle for independence from Turkish rule, a cause that inspired liberal and radical support throughout Europe in the 1820s, helped to prepare the American literary and intellectual community for active involvement in the 1830 liberations. Samuel Gridley Howe, having spent six years fighting with the

Greeks, became so zealous during the Parisian uprising that only Lafayette could persuade him not to risk his life. For Americans generally, Lafayette's leadership linked the revolutions of 1830 with the great Franco-American cause that had been tragically aborted in 1792. James Fenimore Cooper, Samuel F. B. Morse, Howe, and other Americans in Paris joined Lafayette in founding and financing an American-Polish Committee to aid the gallant descendants of Tadeusz Kosciusko and Kazimierz Pulaski, heroes of the American Revolution. Edgar Allan Poe eagerly offered to enlist in the Polish army if Lafayette and the French marched to Warsaw. Parades, rallies, and public demonstrations in the United States raised thousands of dollars that eventually enabled Lafayette's Committee to dispense some relief to the masses of Polish exiles trapped in Prussia, where Howe himself was temporarily imprisoned. Washington Irving, disappointed at missing all the excitement while sojourning in England, rushed to Paris for the coronation of "the Citizen King."[45]

In one of the most penetrating chapters of *Democracy in America,* Tocqueville addressed the common assumption "that there must be a hidden connection and secret link between equality itself and revolutions, so that neither can occur without the other." He concluded, however, that while a democratic society like the United States was hospitable to constant change, motion, and novelty, which Europeans misinterpreted as evidence of instability, "the majority of citizens in a democracy do not see clearly what they could gain by a revolution, but they constantly see a thousand ways in which they could lose by one." Absorbed with their own individual quests for property and self-improvement, wedded stubbornly to certain abstract beliefs and principles, most Americans basically were afraid of revolution. "Almost every revolution which has changed the shape of nations," Tocqueville wrote, echoing a point that had been developed by Aristotle, "has been made to consolidate or destroy inequality." Despite all his talk about equality of condition, Tocqueville knew that some Americans were very rich and some very poor. But in contrast to aristocratic societies, the poor did not form the vast majority of the population. And between the two extremes, "there is an innumerable crowd who are much alike, who, though not exactly rich nor yet quite poor, have enough property to want order and not enough to excite envy." Tocqueville warned that he was not saying "democratic societies are safe from revolutions," and that "if there ever are great revolutions [in the United States], they will be caused by the presence of the blacks upon American soil. That is to say, it will not be the equality of social conditions but rather their inequality which may give rise thereto." In an earlier chapter he had also noted that in the 1790s, "only Washington's immense popularity" had prevented the popular feeling and passion favoring the French Revolution from plunging the nation into war with England, contrary to common sense and obvious national interest.[46]

There is much wisdom in these observations. But reflecting on his visit of 1831, Tocqueville could not foresee the class, ethnic, and ideological differences that would divide Americans over the Mexican War, the Revolution of 1848, and the consequences of industrialism. His dependence on John Marshall's *Life of Washington* prevented him from seeing that there was more than irrational feeling behind American sympathies with the French Revolution, which few Frenchmen could perceive as a direct consequence of the American Revolution. Tocqueville could never really grasp the significance of America's messianic mission, even though he contributed to it in ways that extended from Catharine Beecher's vision of the role of American women to the foreign policy of Woodrow Wilson and the neo-Tocquevilleans of the 1950s and 1960s. By messianic mission I mean the desire to regenerate the United

States by making it the model for revolutionary movements throughout the world. Thus for Karl Heinzen, the German revolutionary and radical abolitionist who immigrated to the United States in 1850 after being banished from numerous European countries, "the United States was a great experiment in liberty and humane culture and a process forever unfinished." Affirming that "as long as there are people in any country who suffer injustice, it is the duty of true radicals to help them," Heinzen linked radical domestic social reform with America's leadership in "the illumination and emancipation of the slavish parts of mankind all over the world."[47]

This millennial mission, though obviously subject to both radical and conservative translations, was essentially an extension of Jefferson's and Paine's revolutionary dreams. In 1848 it led to an outpouring of extravagant praise for what President Polk termed "the sublime spectacle" of "the peaceful rising of the French people, resolved to secure for themselves enlarged liberty . . . and to assert . . . that in this enlightened age man is capable of governing himself." In 1870 it evoked similar rejoicing, if much more subdued, over the downfall of the hated tyrant, Napoleon III, and the proclamation of the Third Republic. In the spring of 1917 it prepared most Americans who read foreign news to believe that Alexander Kerensky's Provisional Government would democratize Russia, perhaps incite revolution in Germany, and transform the Great War into a crusade for a new world order purged of selfish nationalistic ambitions. The Boston Methodist weekly, *Zion's Herald,* voiced the virtually unanimous sentiment of the press, the government, and public meetings: "Autocracy has received its death blow; democracy has triumphed. All of America rejoices to see the dawn of the new day for Russia."[48]

As Tocqueville or John Adams might have predicted, many Americans shrank back in each of these trials as they confronted the realities of the June Days of 1848, the Paris Commune of 1871, crushed by Louis Adolphe Thiers's massacre of over 25,000 Parisians, and the Bolsheviks' seizure of power and conclusion of the Brest-Litovsk Treaty.[49] Beginning in the 1840s, as European radicals increasingly diverged from traditional liberal language and goals, the United States confronted conceptions of equality and class oppression that challenged the fundamental premise that the free ballot and checks on excessive power would ensure maximum opportunity for social progress and self-improvement.

Such challenges, while provoking and nourishing conservative reactions that included pseudo-scientific defenses of inherent inequalities, also altered perceptions of social evil and stimulated significant reforms. When examining American responses to radical revolutions, it is legitimate to dwell on the naive faith of liberals who, as can be seen with the original French and Soviet revolutions, continued to affirm that the democratic spirit of "the people" would prevail and to dismiss the "transitory" or "exaggerated" horrors that could not be fit within their preconceptions of millennial progress. It is no less legitimate to emphasize the loss of confidence and irrational hysteria that could lead to a Red Scare, which as Peter G. Filene puts it, "was Wilsonianism turned inside out, confident messianism become paranoiac, intolerant Americanism seeking to purify the nation of alien and disturbing elements."[50] But these fairly familiar approaches to the culture-bound perception and distortion of foreign realities can also obscure ways in which even misunderstanding has broadened accepted notions of desirable change.

Let me give two quite different but interesting examples of how the misreading of a foreign revolution expanded an American's understanding of equality. Passing over the Marxists and well-known figures like Lincoln Steffens and Thomas Lamont who continued to idealize the Bolsheviks, I turn first to a fascinating article in *The Dial* of December 28, 1918, which argues that analogies between the Russian and French revolutions were superficial and that in "a certain divine sense" "the Russian Revolution parallels the revolt of the thirteen American Colonies. . . . To their respective centuries they have meant the same thing." The author, Lincoln Colcord, a former Washington correspondent for the *Philadelphia Public Ledger*, averred that America's plutocracy had distorted the democratic ideals of the American Revolution, which had sought "to render impossible the domination of a ruling class."[51] Colcord went on to claim that the Soviet system, drawing on the class representation of the ancient village mir, "is nothing but an extension of our own town-meeting principle." Denying that the Bolsheviks were true Marxian socialists, he pictured them confiscating the property of a "small body of Tories" who, as in Revolutionary America, were betraying their country at every turn. Colcord's central point, however, was that the Western democracies could both teach and learn from the Soviets as the world faced economic problems wholly foreign to the Founding Fathers. Instead of sponsoring counterrevolution, the United States should help "Russia to avoid the errors into which Western democracy has fallen in the course of its industrial democracy." In return, the West would learn new methods for achieving equality, for "when we visualize industrial democracy for America, we visualize a state not so far different from the state foreshadowed by the tendencies and potentialities of Soviet Russia."[52]

However naive and misinformed Colcord may have been, this kind of thinking undergirded numerous attempts to revitalize America's democratic heritage and "save" capitalism from its seemingly masochistic inclinations toward self-destruction. Seventy years earlier Frederick Douglass, the greatest black leader of the nineteenth century, made more effective use of the French Revolution of 1848. No better informed than Colcord about a revolution's leaders and disasters, Douglass did know that the provisional government had issued an edict abolishing slavery in all French colonies and, in response to the menacing and rapidly increasing crowds of unemployed, had guaranteed every man the right to work for a living wage, a right symbolically confirmed by the erection of some National Workshops. For Douglass this linkage of the rights of workers and the emancipation of slaves presented an ideal opportunity to excoriate the hypocrisy of Americans who cheered the French for finally following the American model.[53]

Aware that Northern workingmen were increasingly complaining that abolitionists ignored the degradation and suffering of Northern laborers, which could be worse than that of Southern slaves, Douglass rejoiced to see mechanics and laborers in audiences celebrating the French Republic. At one such gathering in Rochester, New York, he praised the "glorious consistency" of the French, who had put "our own country to the blush" by establishing "a government of equality" that recognized the rights of laboring men while also overthrowing slavery "in all her dominions." The news of growing fear among conservative capitalists, and of Southerners suddenly turning against the French Republic, only strengthened Douglass' hand. On August 1, 1848, eleven days after Douglass had helped to carry the contested resolution for woman suffrage at the Seneca Falls Convention, he extolled the French at an interracial commemoration of British West Indian emancipation. The irresistible advance of liberty, equality, and fraternity, he said, has "placed our slaveholding Republic in a dilemma which all the world could see." In other speeches he moved to the central symbol of equality—the language with which the French government had addressed a party of blacks: "'Citizens, friends, brothers!' 'Brothers!' Sir, without this act on the part of the Provisional Government, her democracy or her revolution would have been all a sham."[54]

Sometimes foreign revolutions have reinvigorated Americans' faith in a better world, expanding and redefining the meaning of equality and exposing the hollowness of our own pretensions to social justice. The fear of revolution has often been a spur to progressive reform. At other times, from the Federalist hysteria of the late 1790s to the great Red Scare of 1919–20 and later Cold War decades, foreign revolution has emerged from the shadows wearing all the satanic garb of the original Great American Enemy. From the New Deal to the 1980s, significant reforms have been forced to overcome the stale but remarkably durable accusation of having been inspired by Communists. Americans have made themselves especially vulnerable to this syndrome of "a god who fails" by subordinating world history to their own messianic mission. When other revolutions fail to bring democracy, we tend to conclude that we alone have the capability for safe liberation. Or, on the flip side, foreshadowed by Jefferson himself, when former radicals become disillusioned by a reign of terror or a gulag archipelago, we dismiss them as apostates.

As we approach a new century, indeed a new millennium, we can never forget or justify the unprecedented horrors of the modern era, the tens of millions who have been slaughtered or enslaved as revolutionary zealots pursued final solutions and new world orders. But as the Communist nations begin to reassess their own revolutionary past, nothing can be more disastrous than to proclaim that the cause of American corporate capitalism is now proven to be "the cause of all mankind," that Old World despotism is at last giving way to a modern version of Thomas Paine's "first ripe fruits of American principles transplanted abroad." The values and folkways of one nation can seldom be exported to another. Only time will tell whether the benefits of freedom of expression, civil rights, and free market initiatives can be harmonized with some form of collective responsibility for the health, dignity, and well-being of society's most vulnerable members. The economic and political collapse of Communism in Eastern Europe has coincided with capitalism's continuing failure to resolve the deepening problems of homelessness, poverty, violence, and deficient schooling and health care in virtually every large city in the United States.

Foreign revolutions have helped Americans to tune or adjust the inevitable tension between changing ideals of perfection and present reality. Without a sense of new possibilities in history, without evidence that arrogance and oppression can sometimes be overthrown, the cello strings of American democracy might easily have lost all their capacity for sound. We no longer have time for self-righteousness, cynicism, or the pretense that we have played no part in the twentieth-century's crimes. We are daily made aware of the industrial and technological marvels that have totally transformed the world of Jefferson and Robespierre, providing most Americans with undreamed of comforts, health, conveniences, and knowledge as well as with the more equally shared peril of total annihilation. However one wishes to evaluate this stupendous change, as a historian of slavery and other forms of exploitation and dehumanization, I can only shudder when I think what our world would be like today if industrialization had advanced without political revolutions and the fear of revolutionaries, who, for all their mistakes and self-delusions, perpetuated dreams of equality and social justice.

NOTES

1. *The American Revolution and the Meaning of Equality*

1. *The Papers of Thomas Jefferson,* ed. Julian P. Boyd (Princeton: Princeton University Press, 1950–   ), XVI, 531–532, and footnote. Lafayette, who offered the "main key" and a picture of the Bastille to Washington, "as a son to my adoptive father, as an aid de camp to my General, as a Missionary of Liberty to its Patriarch," entrusted them along with a letter to the care of Thomas Paine, who was traveling from Paris to London. The key was formally presented to the president early in August 1790. Both Lafayette and Paine encouraged the idea that the French Revolution was an extension of the American Revolution. It was to President Washington that Paine dedicated *The Rights of Man,* his vindication of the French Revolution from the aspersions of Edmund Burke.

2. For critical surveys of American responses to foreign revolutions, see Michael H. Hunt, *Ideology and U.S. Foreign Policy* (New Haven: Yale University Press, 1987), chap. 4, "The Perils of Revolution"; and William Appleman Williams, *America Confronts a Revolutionary World: 1776–1976* (New York: William Morrow, 1976). A work that is far more nuanced in its treatment of complex motivations and contradictions is Lloyd C. Gardner, *Safe for Democracy: The Anglo-American Response to Revolution, 1913–1923* (New York: Oxford University Press, 1984). Though hardly writing from a radical perspective, Alexis de Tocqueville tended to belittle the novelty and achievements of the American Revolution. After concluding that the Americans "owed their victory much more to their position than to the valor of their armies or the patriotism of their citizens," he rhetorically exclaimed: "Who would dare to compare the American war to those of the French Revolution or the efforts of the Americans to ours, when France, a prey

to the attacks of all Europe, without money, credit, or allies, threw a twentieth of her population in the face of her enemies, with one hand stifling the devouring flames within her and with the other brandishing the torch around her?" (*Democracy in America,* ed. J. P. Mayer, transl. George Lawrence (Garden City, N.Y.: Doubleday, 1969), p. 113.

3. My composite summary of loyalist arguments is drawn mainly from Mary Beth Norton, *The British-Americans: the Loyalist Exiles in England, 1774–1789* (Boston: Little, Brown, 1972), pp. 130–154. See also Bernard Bailyn, *The Ordeal of Thomas Hutchinson* (Cambridge, Mass.: Harvard University Press, 1974), pp. 35–155, 331–408; Moses Coit Tyler, *The Literary History of the American Revolution, 1763–1783,* 2 vols. (New York: Frederick Unger, reprint, 1957), II, 51–78.

4. For a review of such theories, see Lawrence Stone, "Theories of Revolution," *World Politics* (Princeton: Princeton University Press, 1966), pp. 159–176. Book V of Aristotle's *Politics,* which probably remains the best introduction to the causes of political revolution, points to the inseparable connection between revolutions and conceptions of equality, the theme of my book. According to Aristotle, the "universal and chief cause of revolutionary feeling" is "the desire of equality, when men think that they are equal to others who have more than themselves; or, again, the desire of inequality and superiority, when conceiving themselves to be superior they think that they have not more but the same or less than their inferiors; pretensions which may and may not be just" (*The Student's Oxford Aristotle,* transl. W. D. Ross, vol. 6 [London: Oxford University Press, 1942], 1302a). In his *Old Regime and the Revolution* and especially its unfinished sequel on the French Revolution, Tocqueville merged this theme with the "universal idea of change, coming over everyone without being sought and with no one imagining what the change would be," envisioning an irresistible and continuous historical development toward equality (Tocqueville, "Chapters and Notes for His Unfinished Book on the French Revolution," in *The Two Tocquevilles: Father and Son,* ed. and transl. R. R. Palmer [Princeton: Princeton University Press, 1987], 153–165; Tocqueville, "*The European Revo-*

lution" and Correspondence with Gobineau, ed. and transl. John
Lukacs [Gloucester, Mass.: Peter Smith reprint, 1968], pp. 5–
8, 39–40, 160–172). Despite all his earlier study and theo-
rizing, Tocqueville found himself totally unprepared for the
behavior, speech, and body language of the Montagnards
he confronted in the Constituent Assembly of 1848, to say
nothing of the June Days (Tocqueville, *Recollections,* ed. J. P.
Mayer and A. P. Kerr, transl. George Lawrence [New York:
Doubleday, 1970], pp. 102, 155–166).

5. Bernard Lewis, "Islamic Revolutions," *The New York Review of
Books,* January 21, 1988, pp. 46–50; "Islamic Revolution: An
Exchange," ibid., April 28, 1988, pp. 58–60. The more recent
Salman Rushdie affair, especially Ayatollah Ruhollah Khomeini's order to assassinate a novelist living in England, has
dramatized the confusion and bewilderment of Western liberals
and radicals who have long been accustomed to the censorship
of "counterrevolutionary" writing but who thought of blas-
phemy as being as obsolete as witchcraft.

6. *The New York Times,* May 31, 1988, p. A15; April 28, 1989,
p. A1; May 18, 1989, p. A1; May 20, 1989, p. A1; May 21,
1989, p. A1; June 4, 1989, p. A1; June 6, 1989, p. A1; June 7,
1989, p. A1. In his "Advice to a Young Tradesman," first
printed in 1748, Franklin also affirmed that "CREDIT is
Money," that "Money is of a prolific generating Nature," and
that *"the good Paymaster is Lord of another Man's Purse" (The
Papers of Benjamin Franklin,* ed. Leonard W. Labaree [New
Haven: Yale University Press, 1959–   ], III, 306–307). On
June 15, 1989, in a front-page story on supermarket coupons
being replaced by computerized cash credit, *The New York
Times* quoted Frank Woodward, director of electronic mar-
keting at the Vons Companies, as saying: "The currency of the
1990s is going to be time" (p. A1).

7. As might be expected, numerous columnists and editorial
writers have already seen the "death agonies" of Communism
and the triumph of America's Cold War ideology in the events
of 1989. (See, for example, A. M. Rosenthal, "Beijing and
Moscow," *The New York Times,* June 6, 1989, p. A31; "Communism," *Time,* June 19, 1989, pp. 11–29; and especially "The

Z Document," *The New York Times,* January 4, 1990, p. A23). It is significant that before China's gerontocracy approved the slaughter of at least hundreds of unarmed students, Seymour Martin Lipset allowed his fear of student "uprisings" to override his anti-Communism (see Lipset, "Why Youth Revolt," *The New York Times,* May 24, 1989, op-ed page, and the letter I and four colleagues wrote in response, "Violence of Old Men vs. the Idealism of Youth," ibid., June 7, 1989, p. A26).

8. See especially Williams, *America Confronts a Revolutionary World.*

9. Karl Marx, *The Grundrisse,* ed. and transl. David McLellan (New York: Harper and Row, 1971), pp. 94–95; Karl Marx and Friedrich Engels, "Manifesto of the Communist Party," *The Marx-Engels Reader,* ed. Robert C. Tucker, 2nd ed. (New York: W. W. Norton, 1972), pp. 475–477. While Marx emphasized "the great civilising influence of capital, its production of a stage of society compared with which all earlier stages appear to be merely *local progress* and idolatry of nature," he also predicted of course that this very "universality towards which it is perpetually driving finds limitations in its own nature, which at a certain stage of its development will make it appear as itself the greatest barrier to this tendency, leading thus to its own self-destruction" (Marx, *Grundrisse,* pp. 94–95).

10. V. S. Naipaul, *A Turn in the South* (New York: Knopf, 1989), epigraph.

11. Jefferson to George Mason, February 4, 1791, *Papers of Thomas Jefferson,* ed. Boyd, XIX, 241.

12. Quoted in Gardner, *Safe for Democracy,* pp. 133–134.

13. Larry J. Reynolds, *European Revolutions and the American Literary Renaissance* (New Haven: Yale University Press, 1988), pp. 52–53; Mary L. Dudziak, "Desegregation as a Cold War Imperative," *Stanford Law Review* 41 (November 1988): 113–117.

14. J. H. Elliott, "Revolutions and Continuity in Early Modern History," reprinted in Lawrence Kaplan and Carol Kaplan, eds., *Revolutions: A Comparative Study* (New York: Vintage Books, 1973), pp. 55–56.

15. Edmund Burke, *Reflections on the Revolution in France* (Garden City, N.Y.: Dolphin Books, 1961), pp. 15–17. It is true that

Burke used the word "revolution" to refer to the upheavals of the 1640s, in part because he wished to draw negative analogies with the French Revolution. And as I have already noted, Aristotle devoted considerable attention to the causes of political revolution in various kinds of societies.

16. Robert Middlekauff, *The Glorious Cause: The American Revolution, 1763–1789* (New York: Oxford University Press, 1982), p. 296.

17. Burke, *Reflections,* pp. 22–23, 28–29, 78–80, 84–86. As we shall see, the Great Awakening and the French and Indian Wars encouraged many Americans to look forward to more radical and millennialist "revolutions" than that of 1688.

18. Writing to Jefferson in 1813, Adams claimed that "writings on Government had been not only neglected, but discountenanced and discouraged, through out all Europe, from the Restoration of Charles the Second in England, till the French Revolution commenced. The English Commonwealth, the Fate of Charles 1st, and the military despotism of Cromwell had sickened Mankind with disquisitions on Government to such a degree, that there was scarcely a Man in Europe who had looked into the Subject." This curious argument was intended to explain why Adams' own two works on revolution and constitutional theory were so misunderstood and poorly received (Adams to Jefferson, July 15, 1813, *The Adams-Jefferson Letters,* ed. Lester J. Cappon [2 vols., Chapel Hill: University of North Carolina Press, 1959], II, 357).

19. Raymond Williams, *Keywords: A Vocabulary of Culture and Society* (New York: Oxford University Press, 1976), p. 228. See also Horst Dippel, "The American Revolution and the Modern Concept of 'Revolution,'" in *New Wine in Old Skins: A Comparative View of Socio-Political Structures and Values Affecting the American Revolution,* ed. Erich Angermann, Marie-Luise Frings, and Hermann Wellenreuther (Stuttgart: Ernst Klett Verlag, 1976), pp. 115–129.

20. Charles A. Beard and Mary R. Beard, *The Rise of American Civilization* (New York: Macmillan, 1940), pp. 52–54.

21. I limit my point to the Western world because America's Civil War was dwarfed, in terms of a crude body count, by China's Taiping Rebellion.

22. Tocqueville, *Democracy in America,* ed. Mayer, pp. 9–19, 50–51. As R. R. Palmer has pointed out, Alexis de Tocqueville differed from his father, Hervé, in holding that "the love of liberty had barely reasserted itself in France when it was overwhelmed by another force, the 'violent and inextinguishable hatred for inequality,' which he thought had characterized the French since the Middle Ages" (Introduction to *The Two Tocquevilles,* p. 18).

23. Georges Lefebvre, *The Coming of the French Revolution,* trans. R. R. Palmer (Princeton: Princeton University Press, 1967), p. 209.

24. Edmund S. Morgan, *The Challenge of the American Revolution* (New York: Norton, 1976), p. 194. Morgan's point is extensively elaborated, in somewhat different language, throughout Tocqueville's *Democracy in America.*

25. See especially Stanley N. Katz, "The Strange Birth and Unlikely History of Constitutional Equality," *The Journal of American History* 75 (December 1988): 747–752; Paul Finkelman, "Slavery and the Constitutional Convention: Making a Covenant with Death," in Richard Beeman, Stephen Botein and Edward C. Carter, II, eds. *Beyond Confederation: Origins of the Constitution and American National Identity* (Chapel Hill: University of North Carolina Press, 1987), II, 188–225.

26. *The Collected Works of Abraham Lincoln,* ed. Roy P. Basler, 9 vols. (New Brunswick, N.J.: Rutgers University Press, 1953–1955), II, 385.

27. Morton White, *The Philosophy of the American Revolution* (New York: Oxford University Press, 1978), pp. 62–78, 160–184; *Papers of Thomas Jefferson,* ed. Boyd, I, 423–428. While by no means denying the influence on Jefferson of the Scottish moral sense philosophers, White provides a far more careful and better informed account than Gary Wills, *Inventing America: Jefferson's Declaration of Independence* (Garden City, N.Y.: Doubleday, 1978). It is nevertheless true, as Wills insists, that eighteenth-century beliefs in the uniformity of nature led many philosophers to conclude that at birth men were nearly equal in mental and especially moral capacities, until differentiated by the unequal effects of education and other environmental forces (pp. 207–212). Forrest McDonald points out that Alexander

Hamilton "was one of the few Americans who were willing to tie Locke's epistemology to the question of slavery: Hamilton was convinced that the supposed inferiority of American blacks was a result of conditions under which they lived and that under equal circumstances blacks would prove to be intellectually and socially equal to whites" (McDonald, *Novus Ordo Seclorum: The Intellectual Origins of the Constitution* [Lawrence: University Press of Kansas, 1985], pp. 53–54).

28. White, *Philosophy of the American Revolution,* pp. 68–72. White concludes the sentence with the qualification, "unless God has by a manifest declaration given one man dominion or authority over others," a possibility contemptuously rejected by disciples of the Enlightenment, but a loophole that allowed nineteenth-century proslavery theologians to expand upon the endlessly misinterpreted Curse of Canaan and Hamitic myth.

29. Ibid., pp. 70–71, 266. After the Civil War, judges used the Fourteenth Amendment to sanction a constitutional right to pursue happiness, a concept they interpreted in a great variety of ways (Howard Mumford Jones, *The Pursuit of Happiness* [Cambridge, Mass.: Harvard University Press], pp. 38–47).

30. J. R. Pole, *The Pursuit of Equality in American History* (Berkeley: University of California press, 1978), pp. 22–26.

31. Robert M. Cover, *Justice Accused: Antislavery and the Judicial Process* (New York: Yale University Press, 1975), pp. 42–61; Gordon S. Wood, *The Creation of the American Republic, 1776–1787* (Chapel Hill: University of North Carolina Press, 1969), pp. 70, 133; George M. Fredrickson, *White Supremacy: A Comparative Study in American and South African History* (New York: Oxford University Press, 1981), pp. 143–146; Pole, *Pursuit of Equality,* pp. 49, 126, 128, 135–137. Frank M. Coleman points out that Thomas Hobbes laid the foundation for the claim "that men are fundamentally equal and have equal rights in the covenant relationship. Hobbes stated that no man had a right to reserve rights in the covenant relationship, more than another man, on the presumption of his superiority in intellect, virtue, or wealth" (*Hobbes and America: Exploring the Constitutional Foundations* [Toronto: University of Toronto Press, 1977], pp. 76–77).

32. Bernard Bailyn, *The Ideological Origins of the American Revolu-*

tion (Cambridge, Mass.: Belknap Press of Harvard University Press, 1967), pp. 314–319.

33. Morgan, *Challenge of the American Revolution*, pp. 65, 80–82, 192–95, 211–218; Morgan, *Inventing the People: The Rise of Popular Sovereignty in England and America* (New York: Norton, 1988), pp. 288–306; Ruth H. Bloch, *Visionary Republic: Millennial Themes in American Thought, 1756–1800* (Cambridge: Cambridge University Press, 1985), pp. 53–93; J. G. A. Pocock, *The Machiavellian Moment: Florentine Political Thought and the Atlantic Republican Tradition* (Princeton: Princeton University Press, 1975), pp. 506–552; Wood, *Creation of the American Republic*, pp. 46–124; Robert M. Cover, "Violence and the Word," *The Yale Law Journal* 95 (July 1986): 1601–1609.

34. George Wilson Pierson, *Tocqueville in America*, abridged by Dudley C. Lunt from *Tocqueville and Beaumont in America* (Garden City, N.Y.: Anchor Books, 1959), pp. 40–41.

35. Lev. 19:18; Num. 15:15; Lev. 19:34.

36. Matt. 7:12. For John Adams' application of the Golden Rule, which he termed "the great principle of the law of nature and nations," see White, *Philosophy of the American Revolution*, pp. 59–60.

37. Robert Barclay, *An Apology for the True Christian Divinity: Being an Explanation and Vindication of the Principles and Doctrines of the People Called Quakers* (Providence, 1843), pp. 515–532.

38. Cover, "Violence and the Word," pp. 1601–1629. Drawing on Elaine Scarry's analysis of pain, Cover observes that "the deliberate infliction of pain in order to destroy the victim's normative world and capacity to create shared realities we call torture. . . . The torturer and victim do end up creating their own terrible 'world,' but this world derives its meaning from being imposed upon the ashes of another. The logic of that world is complete domination, though the objective may never be realized." Cover does not specifically point to the connection between domination and inequality. Several historians have commented on the egalitarian impulse that led French Revolutionaries to humiliate the King or to cut out the hearts and drink the blood of aristocrats. But such symbolic rituals

countered inequality with new inequalities. Max Weber's phrase regarding the problem of evil is taken from his "Social Psychology of World Religions" as quoted by Jon P. Gunnemann, *The Moral Meaning of Revolution* (New Haven: Yale University Press, 1979), p. 30.

39. Jean-Jacques Rousseau, *The Social Contract and Discourses,* trans. G. D. H. Cole (London: Everyman's Library, 1930), pp. 5, 9–13, 215, 227–228.

40. For an analysis of Sewell's tract, see David Brion Davis, *The Problem of Slavery in Western Culture* (New York: Oxford University Press, 1988; first published 1966), pp. 344–346. The manuscript containing Lincoln's undated definition of democracy is printed and discussed in *Collected Works of Abraham Lincoln,* ed. Basler, II, 532.

41. John Chester Miller, *The Wolf by the Ears: Thomas Jefferson and Slavery* (New York: Free Press, 1977), p. 41. The French Declaration of the Rights of Man and the Citizen was influenced by George Mason's language in the 1776 Virginia Declaration of Rights (Katz, "Strange Birth and Unlikely History of Constitutional Equality," p. 750).

42. Jefferson to St. George Tucker, August 28, 1797, *The Federal Edition of the Works of Jefferson,* ed. Paul Leicester Ford, 10 vols. (New York, 1892–1899), VII, 167–169.

43. Edmund S. Morgan, "Negrophobia," *The New York Review of Books,* June 16, 1988, p. 27.

44. Bailyn, *Ideological Origins,* pp. 232–246; Davis, *Problem of Slavery,* pp. 273–284; John Locke, *Two Treatises of Government, a Critical Edition with an Introduction and Apparatus Criticus, by Peter Laslett* (Cambridge: Cambridge University Press, 1960), pp. 159, 207–302.

45. Quoted in Alfred F. Young, *The Democratic Republicans of New York: The Origins, 1763–1797* (Chapel Hill: University of North Carolina Press, 1967), p. 141.

46. Henry F. May, *The Enlightenment in America* (New York: Oxford University Press, 1976), pp. 81–82.

47. Drew R. McCoy, *The Elusive Republic: Political Economy in Jeffersonian America* (Chapel Hill: University of North Carolina Press, 1980), p. 237. The perceptive quotation from McCoy's first book must be understood within the context of a pro-

longed historiographical debate regarding the nature and relative importance in the early American Republic of a classical republican ideology, reformulated by the civic humanism of the Italian Renaissance and influenced by the English tradition of "Country" politics exposing the corruptions of a centralizing "Court," as opposed to a more optimistic, open-ended tradition of "liberalism" that was rooted in natural law philosophy and modernized by John Locke and the Scottish moral sense philosophers. Without attempting to summarize the points at issue in this debate, which are defined and redefined in the literature cited at the end of this note, it may be helpful to distinguish two divergent conceptions of equality.

When conceived as an abstract type, classical republicans strove to construct a polity in which all citizens could at least temporarily practice public virtue and avoid corruption by acting in accordance with the public good. Although all men were by nature equal, according to these republicans or civic humanists, fate fortuitously had created wide disparities in their wealth, talents, status, and power. Nevertheless, the privileged and underprivileged remained equal in their capacity for virtue, in their subordination to the public good, and in their vulnerability to corruption if inequality led to self-seeking factions or to ambitious demagogues eager to manipulate dependent followers.

Less pessimistic than the classical republicans about the capriciousness and uncontrollability of fortune and the inevitable cyclicity of social corruption, liberals sought to widen opportunities for both political participation and the acquisition of property. They looked to economic growth and liberation from disabling constraints as the means of eroding inequality and promoting social justice.

In historical reality the republican and liberal traditions often merged in complex ways, sometimes in the mind of a single individual such as Jefferson or Madison. Moreover, the republican or civic humanist fears of self-indulgence and corruption were often expressed in a specifically religious or millennialist vocabulary. If some revisionist historians have erred by mistaking the vibrant, flexible liberalism of the late eighteenth century for the callous, laissez-faire liberalism of the late nineteenth century, others have rediscovered a commitment to equality and civic virtue that overturns traditional assumptions about the conservatism of the American Revolution.

See especially Bailyn, *Ideological Origins;* Wood, *Creation of the American Republic;* Pocock, *Machiavellian Moment,* pp. 208–209, 472–526; Lance Banning, *The Jeffersonian Persuasion* (Ithaca, N.Y.: Cornell University Press, 1978); Dorothy Ross, "The Liberal Tradition Revisited and the Republican Tradition Addressed," in John Higham and Paul K. Conkin, eds., *New Directions in American Intellectual History* (Baltimore: Johns Hopkins Press, 1979), pp. 116–129; Joyce Appleby, "What Is Still American in the Political Philosophy of Thomas Jefferson?" *William and Mary Quarterly* 3rd ser., 39 (April 1982): 287–309; John P. Diggins, *The Lost Soul of American Politics: Virtue, Self-Interest, and the Foundations of Liberalism* (New York: Basic Books, 1984); Joyce Appleby, *Capitalism and a New Social Order: The Republican Vision of the 1790s* (New York: New York University Press, 1983); Lance Banning, "Jeffersonian Ideology Revisited: Liberal and Classical Ideas in the New American Republic," *William and Mary Quarterly* 3rd ser., 43 (January 1986): 3–19; Joyce Appleby, "Republicanism in Old and New Contexts," ibid., pp. 20–34; Ralph Lerner, *The Thinking Revolutionary: Principle and Practice in the New Republic* (Ithaca, N.Y.: Cornell University Press, 1987); Drew R. McCoy, *The Last of the Fathers: James Madison and the Republican Legacy* (Cambridge, Mass.: Harvard University Press, 1989). Linda Colley's analysis of the English Tory Party casts doubt on many of the assumptions American historians have made about British politics in the eighteenth century (*In Defiance of Oligarchy: The Tory Party, 1714–1760* [Cambridge: Cambridge University Press, 1982]).

48. Edmund S. Morgan, *The Challenge of the American Revolution* (New York: Norton, 1976), pp. 215–216.

49. Wood, *Creation of the American Republic,* pp. 72–75; Morgan, "Conflict and Consensus," in *Challenge of the American Revolution,* p. 194.

50. Bailyn, *Ordeal of Thomas Hutchinson,* pp. 67–68, 163, 242–244, 375–377.

51. Adams, much concerned in 1813 about "the impious Idolatry

to Washington," claimed that he had constantly expected "that a Tory History of the Rise and progress of the Revolution would appear," based on "thousands of Letters . . . still concealed." Though he professed to wish for such a history, he could not conceal his anxiety over the judgment of posterity (Adams to Jefferson, July [3], 1813, *Adams-Jefferson Letters,* ed. Cappon, II, 349).

52. Richard Hofstadter, *The American Political Tradition and the Men Who Made It* (New York: Vintage Books, 1974; originally published 1948), pp. 3–21; Reinhold Niebuhr, *The Irony of American History* (New York: Charles Scribner's Sons, 1952), pp. 17–42, 89–108. Both Hofstadter and Niebuhr quote versions of Horace White's remark that the Constitution "is based upon the philosophy of Hobbes and the religion of Calvin" (Hofstadter, *American Political Tradition,* p. 3; Niebuhr, *Irony,* p. 23, footnote).

53. Quoted in *The New York Times,* March 27, 1989, p. A1.

54. Quoted in Gunnemann, *Moral Meaning of Revolution,* pp. 3–4.

55. In this respect nineteenth-century America would seem to differ markedly from the Europe of Alexander Herzen, with its talk of final solutions and "holocausts for the sake of distant goals," to use Isaiah Berlin's phrase ("On the Pursuit of the Ideal," *The New York Review of Books,* March 17, 1988, pp. 11–18). Yet it was in the United States that over 620,000 men died for the seemingly abstract cause of maintaining the Union.

56. Lincoln, *Collected Works,* ed. Basler, II, 385.

57. Eric Foner, *Reconstruction: America's Unfinished Revolution, 1863–1877* (New York: Harper and Row, 1988), pp. 78–81.

58. Quoted in Gunnemann, *Moral Meaning of Revolution,* pp. 72–73.

59. Alfred N. Hunt, *Haiti's Influence on Antebellum America: Slumbering Volcano in the Caribbean* (Baton Rouge: Louisiana State University Press, 1988), pp. 31–36; Albert Hall Bowman, *The Struggle for Neutrality: Franco-American Diplomacy during the Federalist Era* (Knoxville: University of Tennessee Press, 1974), pp. 103–105, 157–158; Thomas O. Ott, *The Haitian Revolution, 1789–1804* (Knoxville: University of Tennessee Press, 1973), pp. 110–114; United States Department of the Navy,

Naval Documents related to the Quasi-War between the United States and France, vol. 7 (Washington: Government Printing Office, 1938), pp. 139–140.

2. *America, France, and the Anxieties of Influence*

1. See especially Orlando Patterson, *Slavery and Social Death: A Comparative Study* (Cambridge, Mass.: Harvard University Press, 1982), pp. 209–296; Suzanne Miers and Igor Kopytoff, eds., *Slavery in Africa: Historical and Anthropological Perspectives* (Madison: University of Wisconsin Press, 1977), pp. 21–55. Although Patterson emphasizes the degradation, parasitism, and general dishonor of slavery, as well as the continuing bonds of dependence that accompany manumission, neither he nor other social scientists I have read explore the implications of these points for the concept of equality.

2. *Décret de la convention nationale, du 16. jour de pluviôse, an second de la République Française, une & indivisible, qui abolit l'esclavage des nègres dans les colonies,* reprinted in *La révolution française et l'abolition de l'esclavage: texts et documents,* 12 vols. (Paris, n.d.), XII, no. 8; Charles Downer Hazen, *Contemporary American Opinion of the French Revolution* (Baltimore, 1897), p. 194.

3. Hazen, *Contemporary American Opinion,* pp. 195–196; Donald H. Stewart, *The Opposition Press of the Federalist Period* (Albany: Albany State University of New York Press, 1969), pp. 115–75; Alfred F. Young, *The Democratic Republicans of New York: The Origins, 1763–1797* (Chapel Hill: University of North Carolina Press, 1967), pp. 349–428; Eugene Perry Link, *Democratic-Republican Societies, 1790–1800* (New York: Columbia University Press, 1942), pp. 44–70, 129, 180–183; Paul Goodman, *The Democratic-Republicans of Massachusetts: Politics in a Young Republic* (Cambridge, Mass.: Harvard University Press, 1964), pp. 52–96. Although Goodman emphasizes that many Massachusetts leaders supported neutrality and had "prudent" second thoughts about the French Revolution by 1793, he also portrays a sharp and continuing ideological polarization in what rapidly became a two-party state.

4. Beatrice F. Hyslop, "American Press, Reports of the French Revolution, 1789–1794," *The New-York Historical Society Quarterly* 42/4 (1958): 329–330, 333–336, 345–346. As Hyslop notes, Holland was the only European country that may have had a more fully developed press than the United States. But the geographic scale was altogether different. In 1791 news coverage of American domestic politics temporarily outweighed foreign news, but the latter took precedence during most of the French Revolution and Vendéen civil war.

5. Gary B. Nash, "The American Clergy and the French Revolution," *William and Mary Quarterly* 3rd ser., 22 (July 1965); 393. In a cabinet paper of April 1793 to President Washington, even Alexander Hamilton used extremely cautious language to question the justice of Louis XVI's execution, and noted that his view differed from that of "a numerous and respectable part, if not . . . a majority, of the people of the United States" (Richard B. Morris, *Alexander Hamilton and the Founding of the Nation* [New York: Dial Press, 1957], pp. 404–405).

6. During the Vendéen war, which, as Donald Greer long ago pointed out, "began as a spontaneous revolt against compulsory military service," soldiers of the French Republican army brutally killed a significant proportion of the peasant population in the western region known as the *Vendée militaire,* although there is still much dispute over the number of victims and their connections with royalists and France's enemies, a politicized controversy that has been reignited by the bicentennial of the French Revolution. (See Donald Greer, *The Incidents of the Terror during the French Revolution* [Cambridge, Mass.: Harvard University Press, 1935], pp. 60–69, 131–166; Charles Tilly, *The Vendée* [Cambridge, Mass.: Harvard University Press, 1964]; Simon Schama, *Citizens: A Chronicle of the French Revolution* [New York: Knopf, 1989], pp. 791–792; Jean-François Fayard, *La justice révolutionnaire: Chronique de la Terreur* [Paris: Editions Robert Laffont, 1987], pp. 12–13 [preface by Pierre Chaunu], pp. 265–270. I have not been able to see a copy of Reynald Secher's polemical and highly controversial *Le génocide Franco-Français: La Vendée-vengé.*)

The French executed approximately 17,000 in the Reign of Terror (Greer, *Incidence of the Terror*, p. 143). Greer provides a detailed breakdown by *département* and occupation; Fayard gives a nearly day-by-day chronicle from March 1793 to August 1794. The American armed forces suffered roughly 9,000 battle deaths in the War of Independence and the War of 1812 (Howard H. Peckham, ed., *The Toll of Independence* [Chicago: University of Chicago Press, 1974], p. 130; *Information Please Almanac: Atlas and Yearbook, 1989,* 42nd ed. [New York: Information Please Almanac, 1989]. For comparative purposes, one may note that Soviet soldiers executed 4,254 Polish officers in the notorious Katyn Massacre (according to Louis Fitzgibbon, former honorary secretary of the British Katyn Memorial Fund; 10,217 others were killed at Dergachi and Bologoye [*New York Times,* May 9, 1989, p. 22]). Between 1889 and 1946 white Americans lynched about 4,000 blacks (Joel Williamson, *The Crucible of Race: Black-White Relations in the American South Since Emancipation* [New York: Oxford University Press, 1984], p. 118). Obviously, body counts can obscure both the horror and historical significance of such killings. The knowledge that Stalin's regime liquidated some twenty million people cannot reduce the stunning impact on the American colonies of five deaths from the Boston Massacre (or the slaying two centuries later of four unarmed students by the Ohio National Guard at Kent State University). Although some Federalist leaders and newspapers condemned the beheading of Louis XVI and subsequent mass executions, large numbers of Americans accepted the violence as the unfortunate cost of liberty and self-defense (see especially Hazen, *Contemporary American Opinion,* pp. 253–263; Hyslop, "American Press Reports," pp. 340–345).

7.   Edward Handler, *America and Europe in the Political Thought of John Adams* (Cambridge, Mass.: Harvard University Press, 1964), pp. 97–98; John Adams to Thomas Jefferson, June 30, 1813; July 13, 1813; July 15, 1813, *The Adams-Jefferson Letters,* ed. Lester J. Cappon, 2 vols. (Chapel Hill: University of North Carolina Press, 1959), II, 346–348, 355–357; *The Diary of William Maclay and Other Notes on Senate Debates,* ed. Kenneth

R. Bowling and Helen E. Veit (Baltimore: Johns Hopkins University Press, 1988), pp. 153, 254. Hamilton and a few other conservatives were not far behind Adams, but they tended to be extremely cautious, at least until France declared war on England in 1793, in expressing skepticism about the Revolution.

8. Jefferson to Madison, November 18, 1788, *The Papers of Thomas Jefferson,* ed. Julian P. Boyd (Princeton: Princeton University Press, 1950–   ), XIV, 188; ibid., I, 124.

9. Gordon S. Wood, *The Creation of the American Republic, 1776–1787* (Chapel Hill: University of North Carolina Press, 1969), pp. 271–273, and passim.

10. To cite only one example of the effects of wishful thinking, James Monroe, writing from Paris in 1795, assured Secretary of State Edmund Randolph that the September Massacres of 1792 and the extermination of the Girondin party "did not proceed from a licentious commotion of the people." The French people, on whom the success of the Revolution would depend according to Monroe, had been kept ignorant of the violent work of outside agents and a few conspirators (Monroe to Randolph, March 6, 1794, *The Writings of James Monroe,* ed. Stanislaus Murray Hamilton, 7 vols. [New York: G. P. Putnam's Sons, 1898–1903], II, 222–226).

11. Historians have tended to overlook, for example, the nature and importance of the public demonstrations that convinced "Citizen Genet" that he could bypass the president and take his case directly to Congress and the people.

12. Ruth Bloch, *Visionary Republic: Millennial Themes in American Thought, 1756–1800* (Cambridge: Cambridge University Press, 1985), pp. 153–162, 202–207; Ruth H. Bloch, "The Social and Political Base of Millennial Literature in Late Eighteenth-Century America," *American Quarterly* 40 (September 1988): 378–396; Lance Banning, *The Jeffersonian Persuasion: Evolution of a Party Ideology* (Ithaca, N.Y.: Cornell University Press, 1978), pp. 238–252; Young, *Democratic Republicans,* pp. 366–467.

13. See especially Banning, *Jeffersonian Persuasion;* Joseph Charles, *The Origins of the American Party System* (New York: Harper,

1961); Drew R. McCoy, *The Elusive Republic: Political Economy in Jeffersonian America* (Chapel Hill: University of North Carolina Press, 1980).

14. R. R. Palmer, *The Age of the Democratic Political Revolution: A Political History of Europe and America, 1760–1800: The Struggle* (Princeton: Princeton University Press, 1964), pp. 55, 522–525. Before Thomas Paine became involved in the French Revolution, he had been an ally of the banker Robert Morris and a defender of the Bank of North America against those he termed "the hot-headed Whigs" (David Freeman Hawke, *Paine* [New York: Harper & Row, 1974], pp. 149–159).

15. Hyslop, "American Press Reports," pp. 341–344, 347. Britain's entry into the war against France in 1793 nourished anti-British feeling, since the French opened their colonial and Continental ports to American commerce and the British retaliated by sinking hundreds of American ships. This naval warfare brought gaps in the European news Americans received. It also contributed to the intense public hostility to John Jay's pro-English treaty of 1794, which the Senate ratified the following year.

16. Handler, *America and Europe,* pp. 73–75; Jefferson to John Jay, May 23, 1788, *Papers of Thomas Jefferson,* XIII, 190; Jefferson to Monroe, August 9, 1788, ibid., 489; Jefferson to Jay, June 29, 1789, ibid., XV, 223.

17. Robert Darnton, "What Was Revolutionary about the French Revolution?" *The New York Review of Books,* January 19, 1989, p. 10.

18. Hazen, *Contemporary American Opinion,* pp. 164–188; Link, *Democratic-Republican Societies,* pp. 44–99, 114–116; Harry Ammon, *The Genet Mission* (New York: Norton, 1973), pp. 51–56; Young, *Democratic Republicans,* pp. 351–375; Stewart, *Opposition Press,* pp. 117–141.

19. Hazen, *Contemporary American Opinion,* pp. 169, 175, 214, 216; Stewart, *Opposition Press,* pp. 117–118; Young, Democratic Republicans, pp. 363–364.

20. Quoted in Hazen, *Contemporary American Opinion,* p. 299. For a modern parallel, stressing that "the Revolution" of the 1960s "meant pretending to be risking something in a com-

pletely risk-free environment. It meant all of the exhilaration of danger without the danger," see Benjamin J. Stein, "Oh, I Miss the Revolution," *The New York Times,* April 4, 1988, op-ed page.

21. Young, *Democratic Republicans,* pp. 351–352; Bloch, *Visionary Republic,* pp. 155, 159; Hazen, *Contemporary American Opinion,* p. 187.

22. Handler, *America and Europe,* p. 102. In 1792 Hamilton assured Colonel Edward Carrington that "I desire above all things to see the equality of political rights, exclusive of all hereditary distinction, firmly established by a practical demonstration of its being consistent with the order and happiness of society (*Alexander Hamilton and the Founding of the Nation,* ed. Richard B. Morris [New York: Dial Press, 1957], p. 124).

23. R. R. Palmer, *The Age of the Democratic Political Revolution: A Political History of Europe and America, 1760–1800: The Challenge* (Princeton: Princeton University Press, 1959); Palmer, ibid.: *The Struggle;* Alexis de Tocqueville, "*The European Revolution*" *and Correspondence with Gobineau,* ed. John Lukacs (Gloucester, Mass.: Peter Smith reprint, 1968); Tocqueville, *The Old Regime and the Revolution,* transl. Stuart Gilbert (Garden City, N.Y.: Doubleday Anchor Books, 1955); Seymour Drescher, "Tocqueville and the French Revolution," *The World and I,* September 1987, pp. 645–661. For the diversity of groups and interests that participated and struggled within the French clubs and societies, see Michael L. Kennedy, *The Jacobin Clubs in the French Revolution: The Middle Years* (Princeton: Princeton University Press, 1988); Isser Woloch, *Jacobin Legacy: The Democratic Movement Under the Directory* (Princeton: Princeton University Press, 1970).

24. For evidence of the diverse nature of Francophile interests, see Young, *Democratic Republicans,* pp. 54–58, 248, 349–350, 371–375; Paul Goodman, *The Democratic-Republicans of Massachusetts: Politics in a Young Republic* (Cambridge, Mass.: Harvard University Press, 1964); Banning, *Jeffersonian Persuasion,* pp. 208–214, 226–245; Link, *Democratic-Republican Societies,* pp. 71–99; Thomas P. Slaughter, *The Whiskey Rebellion: Frontier Epilogue to the American Revolution* (New York: Oxford

University Press, 1986), pp. 127–142; Hyslop, "American Press Reports," pp. 337, 342, 346; Palmer, *Age of the Democratic Revolution: The Challenge*, p. 6.

25. Jefferson to George Mason, February 4, 1791, *Papers of Thomas Jefferson*, XIX, 241.

26. Ammon, *The Genet Mission*, pp. 50–54, 58–79, 96–119, 133–146; Albert Hall Bowman, *The Struggle for Neutrality: Franco-American Diplomacy During the Federalist Era* (Knoxville: University of Tennessee Press, 1974), pp. 76–97; Hazen, *Contemporary American Opinion*, pp. 184–185, 200; Young, *Democratic Republicans*, p. 415. Meade Minnigerode's *Jefferson Friend of France, 1793: The Career of Edmond Charles Genet* (New York: G. P. Putnam's, 1928), draws on the Genet family papers to present a highly critical view of Jefferson's duplicity. Though dismissed as hopelessly biased by Ammon and others, the book helps to balance the pro-Jefferson bias of most American historians and deserves to be evaluated with other evidence.

27. Michael McGiffert, "God's Controversy with Jacobean England," *American Historical Review* 88 (December 1983): 1151–1174; Karen Ordahl Kupperman, "Errand to the Indies: Puritan Colonization from Providence Island through the Western Design," *William and Mary Quarterly* 3rd ser., 45 (January 1988): 70–99; Theodore Dwight Bozeman, "The Puritans' 'Errand into the Wilderness' Reconsidered," *New England Quarterly* 59 (June 1986): 231–251.

28. See especially Bloch, *Visionary Republic*, pp. 22–50, 160–161; Howard Mumford Jones, *America and French Culture, 1750–1848* (Chapel Hill: University of North Carolina Press, 1927), pp. 500–530; David Brion Davis, ed., *The Fear of Conspiracy: Images of Un-American Subversion from the Revolution to the Present* (Ithaca, N.Y.: Cornell University Press, 1971), pp. xiii–xxiv, 23–65; Sacvan Bercovitch, *The American Jeremiad* (Madison: University of Wisconsin Press, 1978), pp. 117–121; Ernest Lee Tuveson, *Redeemer Nation: The Idea of America's Millennial Role* (Chicago: University of Chicago Press, 1968); Nathan O. Hatch, "The Origins of Civil Millennialism in America: New England Clergymen, War with France, and the

Revolution," *William and Mary Quarterly* 3rd ser., 31 (1974): 417; Nathan O. Hatch, *The Sacred Cause of Liberty: Republican Thought and the Millennium in Revolutionary New England* (New Haven: Yale University Press, 1977); James West Davidson, *The Logic of Millennial Thought: Eighteenth-Century New England* (New Haven: Yale University Press, 1977).

29. Benjamin Franklin to David Hartley, February 12, 1778, in *The Papers of Benjamin Franklin,* ed. William B. Willcox et al. (New Haven: 1959–   ), XXV, 651; Henry F. May, *The Enlightenment in America* (New York: Oxford University Press, 1976), p. 116.

30. Hazen, *Contemporary American Opinion,* pp. 62, 68–69.

31. William Gass, "Johns," *The New York Review of Books,* Feb. 2, 1989, p. 22.

32. Quoted in Bloch, *Visionary Republic,* p. 40.

33. Ibid., pp. 3–149; May, *Enlightenment in America,* p. 158.

34. Quoted in Bloch, *Visionary Republic,* pp. 54–98.

35. Rev. 10:4; Bloch, *Visionary Republic,* pp. 158–59. As Bloch points out, millennialists outside New England tended to support the French Revolution until 1798 or even later. Some historians have mistakenly thought that David Osgood, an unorthodox premillennialist who turned against the Revolution in 1795, was typical of the American Protestant clergy as a whole.

36. Bloch, "Social and Political Base of Millennial Literature," pp. 384–396.

37. Nash, "American Clergy and the French Revolution," pp. 393, 395–396; Bloch, *Visionary Republic,* p. 173.

38. Bloch, *Visionary Republic,* pp. 168–170; Hyslop, "American Press Reports," p. 337.

39. Ibid., pp. 162, 171–194; Jefferson to Lafayette, April 2, 1790, *Papers of Thomas Jefferson,* ed. Boyd, XVI, 293; Jefferson to William Stephens Smith, November 13, 1787, ibid., XII, 356; Edmund S. Morgan, *The Gentle Puritan: A Life of Ezra Stiles, 1727–1795* (New Haven: Yale University Press, 1962), pp. 455–461.

40. Jefferson to William Short, January 3, 1793, *The Life and Selected Writings of Thomas Jefferson,* ed. Adrienne Koch and

William Peden (New York: Random House, 1944), pp. 521–522. For a stimulating study of the convergence of religious and rationalist conceptions of utopia, see James Holstun, *A Rational Millennium: Puritan Utopias of Seventeenth-Century England and America* (New York: Oxford University Press, 1987).

41. Woloch, *Jacobin Legacy*, p. 33.

42. Ibid., pp. 30–63; Palmer, *Age of the Democratic Revolution: The Struggle*, pp. 109, 232–243, 327–362.

43. The term "paranoid" proved to be an unfortunate choice, I now believe, because few readers paid heed to Richard Hofstadter's insistence that he was not using the word in a clinical sense but rather "as a historian of art might speak of the baroque or the mannerist style. It is, above all, a way of seeing the world and of expressing oneself" (see Hofstadter, *The Paranoid Style in American Politics* [New York: Alfred A. Knopf, 1965]).

44. David Osgood, *A Discourse, Delivered February 19, 1795, The Day Set Apart by the President for a General Thanksgiving Through the United States* (Boston, 1795), pp. 14–19.

45. See, for example, David Tappan, *A Discourse Delivered in the Chapel of Harvard College, June 19, 1798* (Boston, 1798).

46. David Brion Davis, ed., *The Fear of Conspiracy: Images of Un-American Subversion from the Revolution to the Present* (Ithaca, N.Y.: Cornell University Press, 1971), pp. xiii–xxiv, 35–54. Thomas Hutchinson, who felt that parts of the Declaration were aimed specifically at him, wrote an anonymous pamphlet, *Strictures upon the Declaration of the Congress at Philadelphia, in a Letter to a Noble Lord,* in which he exposed the hypocrisy of the alleged "abuses and usurpations" and asked the Southern delegates "how their constituents justify the depriving more than an hundred thousand Africans of their rights to liberty and *the pursuit of happiness,* and in some degree to their lives, if these rights are so absolutely unalienable" (Bernard Bailyn, *The Ordeal of Thomas Hutchinson* [Cambridge, Mass.: Harvard University Press, 1974], pp. 355–359).

47. John Adams to Benjamin Rush, August 28, 1811, *The Spur of Fame: Dialogues of John Adams and Benjamin Rush, 1805–1813,*

ed. John A. Schutz and Douglass Adair (San Marino, Calif.: The Huntington Library, 1966), p. 191. Belief in the conspiracy of the Illuminati did not end with the Napoleonic period. Robert Welch, the founder of the John Birch Society, traced the origins of Communism to the eighteenth-century Illuminati. In the 1940s Gerald L. K. Smith claimed that Adam Weishaupt, whom Robison and Barruel had portrayed as the Jesuit founder of the Illuminati, was really a Jew who had invented Communism as a means of destroying Christian civilization. According to Smith, the continuing Jewish conspiracy had led to the Protocols of the Elders of Zion, to the assassination of Presidents Lincoln and Kennedy, and to the triumphs of atheistic Communism (Glen Jeansonne, *Gerald L. K. Smith: Minister of Hate* [New Haven: Yale University Press, 1988], pp. 107–109).

48. Matt. 19:21–30, 20:1–16; *The Confessions of Nat Turner, the Leader of the Late Insurrection in Southampton, Va.* (Baltimore, 1831). When Thomas Gray, the white lawyer who transcribed Turner's "confession," asked whether the respondent now found himself mistaken, Turner replied, "Was not Christ crucified?"

49. Alfred N. Hunt, *Haiti's Influence on Antebellum America: Slumbering Volcano in the Caribbean* (Baton Rouge: Louisiana State University Press, 1988), pp. 24–28, 37–83; David Brion Davis, *The Problem of Slavery in the Age of Revolution, 1770–1823* (Ithaca: Cornell University Press, 1975), pp. 186–194, 329–342, 380, 431; Winthrop D. Jordan, *White over Black: American Attitudes Toward the Negro, 1550–1812* (Chapel Hill: University of North Carolina Press, 1968), pp. 375–402; David Patrick Geggus, "British Opinion and the Emergence of Haiti, 1791–1805," in James Walvin, ed., *Slavery and British Society, 1776–1846* (Baton Rouge: Louisiana State University Press, 1982), pp. 137–140; Geggus, "Haiti and the Abolitionists: Opinion, Propaganda and International Politics in Britain and France, 1804–1838," in David Richardson, ed., *Abolition and its Aftermath: The Historical Context, 1790–1916* (London: Frank Cass, 1985), pp. 113–117. David Patrick Geggus states that during the first four years of the rebellion, some 12,000 slaves were taken from Saint-Domingue to the

United States (*Slavery, War, and Revolution: The British Occupation of Saint-Domingue, 1793–1798* [Oxford: Clarendon Press, 1982], p. 305).

50.   Hunt, *Haiti's Influence*, pp. 30–36; Bowman, *The Struggle for Neutrality*, pp. 103–105, 157–158; Thomas O. Ott, *The Haitian Revolution, 1789–1804* (Knoxville: University of Tennessee Press, 1973), pp. 110–114; United States Department of the Navy, *Naval Documents related to the Quasi-War between the United States and France*, vol. 7 (Washington, D.C.: Government Printing Office, 1938), pp. 139–140.

51.   Bishop's text is reprinted by Tim Matthewson, "Abraham Bishop, 'The rights of Black Men,' and the American Reaction to the Haitian Revolution," *Journal of Negro History* 67 (Summer 1982): 148–153. See also Davis, *Problem of Slavery*, pp. 326–328.

52.   Theodore Dwight, *An Oration, Spoken Before "The Connecticut Society, for the Promotion of Freedom and the Relief of Persons Unlawfully Holden in Bondage"* (Hartford, 1794), pp. 10–12.

53.   Ibid., pp. 12–13, 16–21. Dwight quoted the prophecy from the Book of Jeremiah, 34.17.20. By the late 1790s, when his older brother Timothy was president of Yale and leading the crusade in Connecticut against radicalism and religious infidelity, Theodore, according to Leon Howard, "described a Jacobin as a bloodthirsty villain who would find his greatest delight in murdering his mother." Theodore later served as secretary of the secessionist Hartford Convention (Leon Howard, *The Connecticut Wits* [Chicago: University of Chicago Press, 1943], pp. 151, 391. For James Madison, who always condemned slavery in principle and who considered the institution a "blot" or "stain" that "significantly impaired," in Drew R. McCoy's words, "the moral force of America's republican example in the rest of the world," it was not coincidental that the loudest attacks against republican slaveholders came from extreme conservatives and monarchists. (Drew R. McCoy, *The Last of the Fathers: James Madison and the Republican Legacy* [New York: Cambridge University Press, 1989], pp. 260–264).

54.   Julius S. Scott, "Afro-American Slave Revolts in the 1790s," and Douglas R. Egerton, "Gabriel Conspiracy: Uncessful Coda

to the American Revolution," papers presented at the session, "Decades of Unrest: Afro-American Resistance in the Age of Revolution," Annual Meeting of the Organization of American Historians, March 25, 1988; Julius S. Scott, "The Common Wind: Currents of Afro-American Communication in the Era of the Haitian Revolution" (unpublished manuscript kindly sent to me by Professor Scott); Robert S. Starobin, ed., *Denmark Vesey: The Slave Conspiracy of 1822* (Englewood Cliffs, N.J.: Prentice Hall, 1970); Richard C. Wade, "The Vesey Plot: A Reconsideration," *Journal of Southern History* 30 (1964): 143–161; John Lofton, *Denmark Vesey's Revolt: The Slave Plot that Lit a Fuse to Fort Sumter* (Kent, Ohio: Kent State University Press, 1983). In the early 1780s Vesey had worked as a slave in Saint Domingue.

55. Julie Winch, *Philadelphia's Black Elite: Activism, Accommodation, and the Struggle for Autonomy, 1787–1848* (Philadelphia: Temple University Press, 1988), pp. 61, 72–73, 188; John Brown Russwurm, "The Condition and Prospects of Haiti," MS in John Brown Russwurm Papers, Bowdoin College Library; Ira Berlin, *Slaves without Masters: The Free Negro in the Antebellum South* (New York: Pantheon, 1974), pp. 314–315; Hunt, *Haiti's Influence*, pp. 156–182; *David Walker's Appeal, in Four Articles; Together with a Preamble, to the Coloured Citizens of the World, but in Particular, and Very Expressly, to Those of the United States of America*, ed. Charles M. Wiltse (New York: Hill and Wang, 1965; originally published 1829), pp. 20–21. Peter Hinks, in his 1990 Yale Ph.D. dissertation, "'We Must and Shall Be Free': David Walker, Evangelicalism, and Antebellum Black Resistance," points to the influence of the Haitian Revolution on the continuing spirit of black unrest and rebellion in the coastal regions of North and South Carolina in which David Walker grew to manhood.

56. See especially, Robin Blackburn, *The Overthrow of Colonial Slavery, 1776–1848* (London: Verso, 1988), chap. 5, 6, and 9.

3. *The Struggle to Preserve a Revolutionary America*

1. Henry Dwight Sedgwick, Review of "An Anniversary Discourse delivered before the Historical Society . . . showing the

Origin, Progress, Antiquities, Curiosities, and Nature of the Common Law. By William Sampson," *North American Review* 29 (October 1824): 417–421.

2. William Goodell, *Slavery and Anti-Slavery* (New York: William Goodell, 1853), pp. 118–140.

3. *The Diary of John Quincy Adams, 1794–1845,* ed. Allan Nevins (New York: Charles Scribner's, 1951), p. 231; Steven Hahn, *The Roots of Southern Populism: Yeoman Farmers and the Transformation of the Georgia Upcountry, 1850–1890* (New York: Oxford University Press, 1983), p. 86; Michael P. Johnson, *Toward a Patriarchal Republic: The Secession of Georgia* (Baton Rouge: Louisiana State University Press, 1977), pp. 48–51.

4. *The Collected Works of Abraham Lincoln,* ed. Roy P. Basler, 9 vols. (New Brunswick, N.J.: Rutgers University Press, 1955), II, 317–318. Michael Kammen has described the change of the Fourth of July from "a fairly solemn occasion accompanied by church services" to a day "given over to festivities, firecrackers, and gorging (Michael Kammen, *A Season of Youth: The American Revolution and the Historical Imagination* [New York: Alfred A. Knopf, 1978], pp. 54–55).

5. Anne C. Loveland, *Emblem of Liberty: The Image of Lafayette in the American Mind* (Baton Rouge: Louisiana State University Press, 1971), pp. 6–83; Fred Somkin, *Unquiet Eagle: Memory and Desire in the American Idea of Freedom, 1815–1860* [Ithaca, N.Y.: Cornell University Press, 1967], pp. 121–174). Ironically, although Lafayette's reputation suffered in France because he was a nobleman and fled from the country in 1792, after which he was placed in custody by the Hapsburgs, *Time* magazine reports that today in France "polls show that the most revered figure of the [French Revolutionary] era is now the Marquis de Lafayette" (May 1, 1989, p. 50).

6. *Mechanics' Free Press,* October 25, 1828, reprinted in John R. Commons, et al., *Documentary History of American Industrial Society,* 11 vols. (Cleveland: A. H. Clark, 1910–1911), V, 43–45; Thomas Skidmore, *The Rights of Man to Property!* (New York, 1829), pp. 355–358; Sean Wilentz, *Chants Democratic: New York City and the Rise of the American Working Class, 1788–1850* (New York: Oxford University Press, 1984), pp. 61–103, 157–201; Kammen, *Season of Youth,* pp. 44–45.

7. Moses Thatcher, "Address," from *An Abstract of the Proceedings of the Anti-Masonic Convention of Massachusetts* (Boston, 1830), pp. 18–19.

8. Elizabeth Cady Stanton, et al., *History of Woman Suffrage*, 6 vols. (Rochester, N.Y., 1881–1922), I, 58–59.

9. "Declaration of the National Anti-Slavery Convention," *The Abolitionist* I (December 1833): 178.

10. David Walker, *Appeal, in Four Articles; together with a Preamble, to the Coloured Citizens of the World . . .* , ed. Charles M. Wiltse (New York: Hill and Wang, 1965), p. 75; Eric Foner, *Reconstruction: America's Unfinished Revolution, 1863–1877* (New York: Harper & Row, 1988), p. 114.

11. See especially François Furet, *Interpreting the French Revolution,* trans. Elborg Forster (Cambridge: Cambridge University Press, 1981; originally published 1978), p. 12; Robert R. Palmer, Preface to Georges Lefebvre, *The Coming of the French Revolution,* trans. R. R. Palmer (Princeton: Princeton University Press, 1947), p. vii. Although France may no longer be so bitterly divided over its Revolutionary heritage, the 1989 bicentennial has reawakened disputes that Furet and others had consigned to the past (see, for example, Richard Bernstein, "The French Revolution: Right or Wrong?" *The New York Times Book Review,* July 10, 1988, p. 1; *Time,* May 4, 1989, pp. 48–50; *The New York Times,* June 17, 1989, p. A2). In the United States, despite the bitter differences in invoking the Revolution's precedents for conflicting causes virtually everyone hallowed the memory of its leaders and there was no continuing struggle between neo-Tories and the self-appointed heirs of Sam Adams and Patrick Henry.

12. John C. Calhoun, "Speech on Henry Clay's Compromise Resolution on the Bill to Admit California, March 4, 1850," in John M. Anderson, ed. *Calhoun: Basic Documents* (State College, Pa.: Bald Eagle Press, 1952), pp. 306–312; Abraham Lincoln to Joshua F. Speed, August 24, 1855, *Collected Works,* II, 323.

13. See especially Merrill D. Peterson, *The Jefferson Image in the American Mind* (New York: Oxford University Press, 1960). As Peterson shows, some conservatives have portrayed Jefferson's thought as the Americanization of an Anglo-Saxon tradi-

tion of political liberty, uncontaminated by visionary or radical French philosophy, while other conservatives, especially in the antebellum South, repudiated Jefferson precisely because his doctrines seemed to justify revolutionary change, including slave emancipation. In the late 1930s and early 1940s, when the Communist Party proclaimed that "Communism is Twentieth Century Americanism," Jefferson was hailed as a precursor to Marx and Lenin, only a step below the more plebeian Tom Paine in the pantheon of heroes. His support for revolutionary France was supposed to encourage twentieth-century Americans to support Russia's struggle against fascism (Peterson, *Jefferson Image,* pp. 366–368). More recently, Richard K. Matthews has challenged most conventional views by arguing that "Jefferson was America's first and foremost advocate of permanent revolution," whose political system "specifically calls for mass participatory democracy" (*The Radical Politics of Thomas Jefferson: A Revisionist View* [Lawrence: University of Kansas Press, 1984], pp. 125–126).

14. John Adams to Thomas Jefferson, July 13, 1813, *The Adams-Jefferson Letters,* ed. Lester J. Cappon, 2 vols. (Chapel Hill: University of North Carolina Press, 1959), II, 356; Jefferson to James Madison, January 30, 1787, *The Papers of Thomas Jefferson,* ed. Julian P. Boyd (Princeton: Princeton University Press, 1950–), XI, 93; Jefferson to William Stephens Smith, November 13, 1787, ibid., XII, 356; Jefferson to Lafayette, April 2, 1790, ibid., XVI, 292. Adams asserted that the French Revolution was the first issue of any importance on which he and Jefferson had differed. He told Jefferson that he would forfeit his life if Jefferson could find one sentence Adams had written in his two controversial books that could be fairly construed as favoring "the introduction of hereditary Monarchy or Aristocracy into America."

15. John Adams to Benjamin Rush, December 25, 1811, *The Spur of Fame: Dialogues of John Adams and Benjamin Rush, 1805–1813,* ed. John A. Schutz and Douglass Adair (San Marino, Calif.: The Huntington Library, 1966), pp. 200–202.

16. Adams to Jefferson, May 11, 1794, *Adams-Jefferson Letters,* ed. Cappon, II, 255.

17. Adams to Jefferson, June 30, 1813, ibid., II, 346–347. The

surviving circular letters sent by congressmen are bitterly partisan and much concerned with foreign affairs during Adams' administration. In 1797 and 1798, for example, John Clopton, Anthony New, and Samuel Cabell of Virginia accused Adams of deliberately deceiving the people, violating the Constitution, and in effect declaring war on France. But these pro-French reports were matched by the extremely Francophobe letters of Robert Goodloe Harper, of South Carolina. The recently published collection contains no circular letters that would seem to substantiate Adams' suspicions of incitement to riot. See *Circular Letters of Congressmen to Their Constituents, 1789–1829,* ed. Noble E. Cunningham, Jr., 3 vols. (Chapel Hill: University of North Carolina Press, 1978), I, 72–76, 87, 94–98, 103–104, 107–110, 112–113, 115, 123, 191–192.

18. Adams was extremely cautious on the issue of slavery. It was only during the Missouri crisis, after Jefferson had tried to link the antislavery cause with religious bigotry and had defined "the real question" as one of civil war—"Are our slaves to be presented with freedom and a dagger?"—that Adams responded: "Slavery in this Country I have seen hanging over it like a black cloud for half a Century. If I were as drunk with enthusiasm as Swedenborg or Westley, I might probably say I had seen Armies of Negroes marching and countermarching in the air, shining in Armour. I have been so terrified with this Phenomenon that I constantly said in former times to the Southern Gentlemen, I cannot comprehend this object; I must leave it to you. I will vote for forceing no measure against your judgements. What we are to see, *God* knows, and I leave it to him, and his agents in posterity. I have none of the genius of Franklin, to invent a rod to draw from the cloud its Thunder and lightning" (Jefferson to Adams, January 22, 1821; Adams to Jefferson, February 3, 1821, *Adams-Jefferson Letters,* ed. Cappon, II, 569–571).

19. Adams to Jefferson, July 15, 1813, ibid., II, 357.

20. Jefferson to the Marquis de Lafayette, February 14, 1815, *The Works of Thomas Jefferson,* ed. Paul Leicester Ford, 12 vols. (New York: G. P. Putnam's Sons, 1904–05), XI, 454–458. When writing to Lafayette, Jefferson chose to forget his defense of the Jacobins and recalled only his earlier caution.

21. Jefferson to Adams, January 11, 1816, *Adams-Jefferson Letters,* ed. Cappon, II, 458–460.

22. Ibid.

23. Adams to Jefferson, February 2, 1816, ibid., p. 461.

24. Ibid.; Adams to Jefferson, December 16, 1816, ibid., p. 502.

25. Adams to Jefferson, August 15, 1823, ibid., pp. 594–595.

26. Adams to Jefferson, February 2, 1816; Adams to Jefferson, November 4, 1816, ibid., pp. 462, 494.

27. Adams to Jefferson, November 15, 1813, ibid., pp. 398–399.

28. Ibid.; Jefferson to Adams, September 4, 1823, ibid., p. 596; Adams to Jefferson, September 18, 1823, ibid., p. 598. Perhaps because he was replying to Jefferson, Adams wrote: "It is melancholy to contemplate the cruel wars, dessolutions of Countries, and ocians of blood which must occure, before rational principles, and rational systems of Government can prevail and be established. But as these are inevitable we must content ourselves with the consolations which you from sound and sure reasons so clearly suggest. Thes[e] hopes are as well founded as our fears of the contrary evils; on the whole, the prospect is cheering."

29. Jefferson to Adams, April 8, 1816, ibid., p. 467.

30. Jefferson to Adams, January 22, 1821; September 4, 1823, ibid., pp. 570, 596.

31. Jefferson to Adams, January 22, 1821, ibid., p. 570.

32. Jefferson to Adams, September 12, 1821; September 4, 1823, ibid., pp. 575, 596–597.

33. Jerry Israel, *Progressivism and the Open Door: America and China, 1905–1921* (Pittsburgh: University of Pittsburgh Press, 1971), p. 101; Jonathan D. Spence, *The Gate of Heavenly Peace: The Chinese and Their Revolution, 1895–1980* (New York: Viking Press, 1981), pp. 81–84, 93–100, 226; Michael V. Metallo, "American Missionaries, Sun Yat-sen, and the Chinese Revolution," *Pacific Historical Review* 47 (Spring 1978): 261–282. Bryan chose Yuan Shikai because he had been named provisional president of China after the last Manchu ruler had abdicated.

34. James Reed, *The Missionary Mind and American East Asia Policy, 1911–1915* (Cambridge, Mass.: Harvard University Press, 1983), pp. 121–126.

35. Charles Carroll Griffin, *The United States and the Disruption of the Spanish Empire, 1810–1822: A Study of the Relations of the United States with Spain and with the Rebel Spanish Colonies* (New York: Columbia University Press, 1937), pp. 46–51, 122–157; Richard E. Welch, Jr., *Response to Revolution: The United States and the Cuban Revolution, 1959–1961* (Chapel Hill: University of North Carolina Press, 1985), pp. 161–162. Much of the mainstream American press began to turn against the Cuban Revolution in the summer and fall of 1959.

36. Ronald Steel, "The Strange Case of William Bullitt," *The New York Review of Books,* September 29, 1988, p. 15; Beatrice Farnsworth, *William C. Bullitt and the Soviet Union* (Bloomington: Indiana University Press, 1967), pp. 32–54; Lloyd C. Gardner, *Safe for Democracy: The Anglo-American Response to Revolution, 1913–1923* (New York: Oxford University Press, 1984), pp. 240–242; Eugene N. Curtis, "American Opinion of the French Nineteenth-Century Revolutions," *American Historical Review* 29 (January 1924): 255. Bullitt's remark to Steffens has almost always been attributed to Steffens himself. Buchanan also wrote Rush that President Polk would have been displeased if the representative of any other nation had "preceded you in this good work" (John Gerow Gazley, *American Opinion of German Unification, 1848–1871* [New York: Columbia University Press, 1926], p. 235).

37. Francis Bowen, the editor of the *North American Review,* tried to alert Americans to the fact that Kossuth and the Hungarian rebels had ruthlessly suppressed their Slav neighbors (Merle Curti, "The Impact of the Revolutions of 1848 on American Thought," *Proceedings of the American Philosophical Society* 93 [June 1949]: 213–214).

38. Drew R. McCoy, *The Last of the Fathers: James Madison and the Republican Legacy* (New York: Cambridge University Press, 1989), p. 262.

39. Ibid., pp. 262–263.

40. *Annals of Congress,* 16th Cong., 1st sess., 2223–2229; "Speech on South American Independence from May 10, 1820," in *The Papers of Henry Clay,* ed. James F. Hopkins (Lexington: University of Kentucky Press, 1959–), II, 858; Merrill D. Peterson, *The Great Triumvirate: Webster, Clay, and Calhoun*

(New York: Oxford University Press, 1987), pp. 52–53. The full congressional debate involving Clay's speech of 1820 was not recorded in the *Annals*.

41. For a recent overview of slave emancipation during the wars of independence, see Robin Blackburn, *The Overthrow of Colonial Slavery, 1776–1848* (London: Verso, 1988), chap. 9.

42. Griffin, *United States and the Disruption of the Spanish Empire*, p. 131; Clement Eaton, *Henry Clay and the Art of American Politics* (Boston: Little, Brown, 1957), pp. 34–47; Peterson, *Great Triumvirate*, pp. 54–55. In Congress, however, Clay's early proposals were overwhelmingly defeated, and it was not until 1822 that the United States recognized the Latin American republics. If Clay was primarily interested in opening new markets for trade, his rhetoric continued to stress the Latin Americans' capacity for self-government and the similarity of their own struggles with America's War of Independence.

43. E. J. Hobsbawm, *The Age of Revolution, 1789–1848* (New York: Mentor paperback ed., 1962), pp. 137–164.

44. Curtis, "American Opinion," pp. 249–250; Robert O. Paxton, "The Divided Liberal," *The New York Review of Books*, March 2, 1989, p. 17.

45. Paul Constantine Pappas, *The United States and the Greek War for Independence, 1821–1828* (New York: Columbia University Press, 1985), pp. 26–43; Edward Mead Earle, "American Interest in the Greek Cause, 1821–1827," *American Historical Review* 33 (October 1927): 45–63; Curtis, "American Opinion," pp. 251–254; Jerzy Jan Lerski, *A Polish Chapter in Jacksonian America: The United States and the Polish Exiles of 1831* (Madison: University of Wisconsin Press, 1958), pp. 14–76; Loveland, *Emblem of Liberty*, pp. 118–132.

46. Alexis de Tocqueville, *Democracy in America*, ed. J. P. Mayer, transl. George Lawrence (Garden City, N.Y.: Anchor Books, 1969), pp. 229–230, 634–645. As I mentioned in Chapter 1, note 4, Book V of Aristotle's *Politics* is devoted to the theme of revolution and inequality.

47. Carl Wittke, *Against the Current: The Life of Carl Heinzen* (Chicago: University of Chicago Press, 1945), pp. 207, 251, 253.

48. Curtis, "American Opinion," pp. 255, 263–270; Arthur J.

May, "The United States and the Mid-Century Revolutions," in François Fejtö, ed., *The Opening of an Era: 1848: An Historical Symposium* (New York: Grosset & Dunlap, 1973; first published 1948), pp. 204–213; "The Russian Revolution: The History of Four Days," *Outlook* 115 (March 28, 1917): 544–545; George Kennan, "The Victory of the Russian People," ibid., 546–547; "New Russia and the War, Distant Effects of the Russian Earthquake," *The Nation* 104 (March 1917): 330–331; Arthur W. Thompson and Robert A. Hart, *The Uncertain Crusade: America and the Russian Revolution of 1905* (Amherst: University of Massachusetts Press, 1970); John Lewis Gaddis, *Russia, the Soviet Union, and the United States: An Interpretive Essay* (New York: Alfred A. Knopf, 1978), pp. 57–72; Christopher Lasch, *The American Liberals and the Russian Revolution* (New York: Columbia University Press, 1962), pp. 27–56; Gardner, *Safe for Democracy*, pp. 131–37; Peter G. Filene, *Americans and the Soviet Experiment, 1917–1933* (Cambridge, Mass.: Harvard University Press, 1967); pp. 9–20.

49. Curtis, "American Opinion," pp. 258–270; George L. Cherry, "American Metropolitan Press Reaction to the Paris Commune of 1871," *Mid-America* 32 (January 1950): 3–12; *The Outlook* 117 (December 5, 1917): 551; "The Russian Chaos," *The American Review of Reviews* 58 (October 1918): 348–349; George F. Kennan, *Soviet-American Relations, 1917–1920: Russia Leaves the War* (Princeton: Princeton University Press, 1956), pp. 364–377; Lasch, *American Liberals*, pp. 57–82, 127–131.

50. Filene, *Americans and the Soviet Experiment*, p. 63. As Filene shows, even after Russia withdrew from the war, businessmen, religious leaders, and numerous public meetings called for economic and spiritual aid to the Russian people, who could not be abandoned now that they had been freed from czarist despotism (pp. 17–24, 56). As David M. Kennedy suggests, the propaganda and hate originally directed against the Germans prepared the way for the obsessions and terror of the Great Red Scare (David M. Kennedy, *Over Here: The First World War and American Society* [New York: Oxford University Press, 1980]).

51. Lincoln Colcord, "Soviet Russia and the American Revolu-

tion," *The Dial* 65 (December 28, 1918): 591–595. In March 1918 Colcord had aided William C. Bullitt and William Boyce Thompson in persuading Colonel Edward House and President Wilson that a cordial presidential message should be sent to the "people of Russia through the Soviet Congress," a message which in effect identified Lenin and the Soviet regime with "the whole struggle for freedom" that was supposedly threatened by Germany. The message, drafted by Bullitt on March 9, was intended to persuade the Soviet Congress to withhold Ratification of the Brest-Litovsk Treaty. The Soviet Congress, which ratified the treaty on March 16, sent a deliberately insulting reply that condemned "the imperialist war" and called on the "toiling masses" of all bourgeois countries to overthrow their governments (Kennan, *Russia Leaves the War,* pp. 509–513; Farnsworth, *William C. Bullitt,* pp. 23–24). Neither Wilson nor his advisers were fully aware that German leaders had devised the plan to transport Lenin from Zurich to Russia or that Lenin was, as Sebastian Haffner puts it, "the German secret- and wonder-weapon, the political atom bomb of the First World War" (Quoted by Gordon A. Craig from Haffner, *Der Teufelspakt: Die deutsch-russischen Beziehungen vom Ersten zum Zweiten Weltkrieg,* in "Dangerous Liaisons," *The New York Review of Books,* March 30, 1989, p. 15).

52. Colcord, "Soviet Russia," p. 595.
53. Frederick Douglass, "The Triumphs and Challenges of the Abolitionist Crusade: An Address Delivered in New York, New York, on 9 May 1848," *The Frederick Douglass Papers,* series One: *Speeches, Debates, and Interviews,* ed. John W. Blassingame (New Haven: Yale University Press, 1979–   ), II, 122–123, 127; "The Slaves' Right to Revolt: An Address Delivered in Boston, Massachusetts, on 30 May 1848," ibid., pp. 131–132; "A Day, a Deed, an Event, Glorious in the Annals of Philanthropy: An Address Delivered in Rochester, New York, on 1 August 1848," ibid., pp. 136–141. As Georges Duveau points out, the cooperative workshops controlled by workers' associations that had been envisioned by Louis Blanc "bore no relation to the National Workshops, which were simply ordinary charity institutions" in which the unemployed "spent

most of their time playing billiards and making speeches in praise of the social-democratic Republic." Wholly inadequate as a solution to the economic crisis and massive unemployment, the Parisian Workshops did briefly provide a potential army to crush antigovernment extremists (Georges Duveau, *1848: The Making of a Revolution,* transl. Anne Carter [Cambridge, Mass.: Harvard University Press, 1967], pp. 64–70.

54. Frederick Douglass, "The 1848 Revolution in France: An Address Delivered in Rochester, New York, on 27 April 1848," *Frederick Douglass Papers,* II, 115–117; and Douglass' other speeches cited in note 53.

INDEX